Nothing Out of This World
Cuban Poetry 1952–2000

Nothing Out of This World
Cuban Poetry 1952–2000

Translated and edited by
Katherine M. Hedeen

Smokestack Books
1 Lake Terrace, Grewelthorpe, Ripon HG4 3BU
e-mail: info@smokestack-books.co.uk
www.smokestack-books.co.uk

Translations copyright Katherine M. Hedeen.
Introduction copyright Víctor Rodríguez Núñez.

ISBN 9780993454738

Smokestack Books is represented
by Inpress Ltd

This book has been selected to receive financial assistance from English PEN's "PEN Translates!" programme, supported by Arts Council England. English PEN exists to promote literature and our understanding of it, to uphold writers' freedoms around the world, to campaign against the persecution and imprisonment of writers for stating their views, and to promote the friendly co-operation of writers and the free exchange of ideas. www.englishpen.org.

Contents

Víctor Rodríguez Núñez
   Introduction   10
Fina García-Marruz
   There's No Time to Start from the Beginning...   37
   Our Indians   38
   The Solemn Lessons (1 and 6)   40
Carilda Oliver Labra
   The Dead Neighbour Woman   42
   To Hope I Return, to the Wood   43
   Lost Words   44
Lorenzo García Vega
   Reina Street   45
   Dry Rain   46
   What I'm Being   47
Roberto Friol
   Mysteries   48
   The Double Face   49
   Before a Chinese Pencil   50
Francisco de Oraá
   As if They Kicked You Out of Sleep   51
   Dry   52
   On Three Photos of Mella   53
Pablo Armando Fernández
   The Rooster of Pomander Walk (V and XI)   55
   Nihil Obstat   57
   Salt of Memory   58
Fayad Jamís
   Sleepless Man's Rounds (III and V)   59
   For this Freedom   60
   Better to Get Up   61
Roberto Fernández Retamar
   The Ugly Ones   62
   You Were Right, Tallet: We Are Men of Transition   63
Heberto Padilla
   Cuban Poets No Longer Dream   66

The Man on the Edge	67
Offside	68
César López	
The tablecloths and sheets…	70
Minute, tiny park, sombre and quiet…	73
Rafael Alcides Pérez	
The Grateful One	75
A Man and a Woman	76
Nobody	77
Antón Arrufat	
Metals	78
At the Son's Door	79
Apology in Detail	80
Manuel Díaz Martínez	
Leave	82
The House	83
Immortals	84
José Kozer	
My Father, Who Is Still Alive	86
On the Nation	87
Miguel Barnet	
Revolution	89
Orishas	90
Miami	92
Luis Rogelio Nogueras	
P4R	94
Joe Bell/The Inspector's Last Case	97
Nancy Morejón	
Mutisms (IV)	99
Carpet	100
The Golden Chair	101
Raúl Rivero	
Pardon This Slight Distraction	103
Death Suite	104
Lina de Feria	
if those who don't want to understand me…	107
From María García Granados to José Martí	108
The Mudslide and the Burial (II)	109

Raúl Hernández Novás
  She watched the tall flamboyant trees catch fire...   110
  The Sun in the Snow   111
  He Has Told Me   113
Luis Lorente
  Fable Rain   114
  Under the Wheels   117
José Pérez Olivares
  The Magician (Arcana I)   118
  Reflections by the Painter James Ensor   119
  Reflection on the Kiss of Judas   121
Soleida Ríos
  Flows (2, 5, 8, 11, and 12)   122
  Tuesday the 13th in the Sargasso Sea   124
Reina María Rodríguez
  Regrets for a White Lamb   126
  The Women Write Love Letters   127
  The Winter Garden Photograph   128
Alex Fleites
  Cancelled Poem   129
  Simple Story   131
Víctor Rodríguez Núñez
  Prologue – to Rafael Alberti's *The Lost Grove*   132
  Marco Polo's Dilemma   133
  Praise for the Neutrino   134
Ángel Escobar
  A Question   136
  7:15 a.m.   137
  Sense   138
Ramón Fernández-Larrea
  Transitory Poem   139
  Reina Street's Arcades   140
Roberto Méndez
  I Can Open My Eyes   143
  The Stellar   144
  Transfiguration   146
Sigfredo Ariel
  En C'est Temps La   147

(Other) Lost Labours of Love	149
Provisions	150
Juan Carlos Pérez Flores	
The Stranger	151
Page in Homage to the Goliard Poets	152
NASA	153
Alberto Rodríguez Tosca	
Pandemonium of Freedom	154
All the Happiness Is in a Telephone Booth	155
Carlos Augusto Alfonso	
Stockholm Syndrome	158
The Dog	160
Labarum	162
Ricardo Alberto Pérez	
Critical Essay on My Father's Hands	163
The Painting Where the Dog Was	164
The Poem's Words	165
Omar Pérez López	
Mules and Knights	166
Breadcrumb Soup	167
Evangelicals	168
Damaris Calderón	
A Woman Alone and Bitter	169
Mezcal	170
Syllables. Ecce homo	171

Introduction:
Nothing Out of This World or
Dialogic Poetry in Cuba

I

In the introduction to his celebrated anthology *Cincuenta años de poesía cubana* [Fifty Years of Cuban Poetry] (Havana: Dirección de Cultura del Ministerio de Educación, 1952), Cintio Vitier notes that in 1902, 'the rise of the Republic surprises our dispersed, disoriented poetry' (Introducción 1).[1] At the end of the nineteenth century, José Martí and Julián del Casal have died, the island's greatest poets and founders of the literary movement *el modernismo*.[2] Their poetic subjects are not opposed, as conventional criticism has held, but rather complement one another. The former challenges Spanish colonialism, then in decline, and the latter the ascending order of creole elites.[3] During the first ten years of the new century, poetic production is 'undefined and naive, like the Republic itself, with romantic, *modernista*, and decadent qualities' (Vitier Introducción 1). This lamentable state will be modified 'by the successive appearance of three books written from Cuba's inland. They are *Arabescos mentales* (1913) by Regino E. Boti, *Ala* (1915) by Agustín Acosta, and *Versos precursores* (1917) by José Manuel Poveda' (Vitier Introducción 1). While Boti and Poveda 'continue a *modernista* vein and then immediately transcend it to reveal a rescuing of the idea of poetry as an autonomous verbal creation,' Acosta 'demonstrates a simpler lyrical tone, malleable and 'human', soon aware of patriotic and historical concerns' (Vitier Introducción 1).

In the twenties, according to Vitier, the Cuban nation 'exposes, on the one hand, its major economic error, the unstableness of its independence; and on the other, it becomes bureaucratized and begins to focus on the political waterwheel. Poets' reactions correspond to these two faces of reality' (Introducción 2). Among those who participate in resisting the Republic's senselessness, the critic emphasizes José Z. Tallet, whose work 'deals with the urban experience of disappointment and irony when in the presence of mediocrity, made up of gestures devoid of substance' (Introducción 2); Dulce María Loynaz, with her intimism 'centered on the delicacies and hints of feeling which will close [...] the post-*modernista* era,[4] fractured at last by new concerns where European avant-garde trends will coincide with the revolutionary unrest brought about by the fall of General Gerardo Machado's tyrannical regimen' in 1933 (Introducción 2); and lastly Regino Pedroso, whose craft evolves 'from the last waves of *modernismo* toward the avant-garde and social unrest' (Introducción 2) – and who will create in *Nosotros* (1933) a subject who confronts class oppression.

In this process of renovation, the *Revista de Avance* figures prominently. According to Vitier, 'a new period begins in our literature. Polemical, aggressive, and ironic, its main purpose is to do away with provincial tastes and outdated attitudes' (Introducción 2). For the critic, the impact of this journal is 'quite considerable and is revealed in three ways: "pure" poetry, "black" or "mulatto" poetry, and "social" poetry'. The first produces three initial books of an extraordinary quality: *Poemas en menguante* (1928) by Mariano Brull, *Trópico* (1930) by Eugenio Florit, and *Júbilo y fuga* (1931) by Emilio Ballagas.[5] The last two are exemplarily brought together in Nicolás Guillén's *Sóngoro cosongo* (1931)' (Introducción 3). This last poet 'is able to go beyond the speculations of imported European approaches to *negrismo* and numerous superficial aspects of the local treatment of the topic, to form a folkloric, social, free poetry, with a refined universality, based on an inner communication with Afro-Cuban emotion and music' (Vitier Introducción 3). In later collections, Guillén constructs an ethnic subject who confronts the concept of nation as defined by the elite classes in power.

For Vitier, the journals founded by José Lezama Lima and the poets who follow him – *Verbum* (1937), *Espuela de Plata* (1939), *Clavileño* (1942), *Poeta* (1942), *Nadie Parecía* (1942), and above all *Orígenes* (1944-1956) – 'mean an effective change in lyrical sensibility and set themselves apart with two main features: they are not polemical (at least in an explicit way) and what dominates their core is poetry' (Introducción 4). The critic emphasizes the 'creative absorption of a generation now uninterested in post-Machado political comedy, and focused not as much on 'advancement' as on submerging themselves in search of 'origins' (dark and unreachable, as the deepest foundations of life always are) of our creative sensibility' (Introducción 4). Among the poets of *Orígenes* who stand out are, along with Lezama Lima, Gastón Baquero, Virgilio Piñera, Eliseo Diego, and Vitier himself – who constructs in *Extrañeza de estar* (1944) a subject opposed to the neocolonial order.[6] A lyrical poetry from the period that also stands out and doesn't escape Vitier's critical gaze, is that of his contemporary Samuel Feijóo. In *Orígenes* coexist not only dissimilar but often times opposing worldviews and poetics; among them the dialogic poetry the present selection attempts to document.

And so in 1959 the Revolution in no way surprises Cuban poetry as 'dispersed' or 'disoriented.' It had already amassed a vast experience in the representation of the system of social subordinations it attempts to overturn – nation, social class, gender, ethnicity, sexual orientation. It had participated in the struggles for the transformation of a deformed, dependent capitalism, which enters into crisis in Cuba in the fifties. And in that social-cultural process, it had decolonized itself, in content and in form. Ultimately, Cuban poetry was revolutionary before the Revolution; it has continued to be in the midst of profound transformations made since 1959, and despite the paradoxical distrust of revolutionary power; and it still is after the decline of the Revolution that begins in the nineties. A revolutionary poetry not because it's realist, and much less Socialist Realist; revolutionary not because it's colloquial but because it renounces solipsism in diverse ways. For that reason, Cuban poets have no reason to feel, throughout the second half of the twentieth century, any guilt. Representation, when it's not limited to the phenomenal, implies subversion; and intellectuals' social participation is carried out, principally, through their cultural production.

II

When commenting on *Con figura de gente y en uso de razón* (1968) – by the non-colloquial Cuban poet Francisco de Oraá – Vitier points out in particular its break with solipsism, whose context is 'market, usury, profit' (Solipsismo 294), and consists 'mostly [of being] *separated* from oneself, from others' (Solipsismo 291). Oraá's work is a case of dialogic poetry, whose base is the awareness of otherness, the decision by the author to become, in the words of Bakhtin, 'another in relation to himself' (15). For the Russian thinker, '[o]ne must come to feel at home in the world of other people [...] in order to be able to go on from confession – to make objective aesthetic contemplation, from questions about meaning and searchings for meaning – to the world as a beautiful given' (111). One must understand that 'it is about the other that all the stories have been composed, all the books have been written, all the tears have been shed; it is to him that all the monuments have been erected [...] it is only others who are known, remembered, and recreated by productive memory, so that my own memory of objects, of the world, and of life could also become an artistic memory' (Bakhtin 111-112). Ultimately, the dialogic author is aware that 'I am not the hero of my own life' (Bakhtin 112), and that 'aesthetic contemplation – co-creation [with the reader, the other's other] – is immanent to a work of art' (Bakhtin 148-49).

As for poetry, Bakhtin points out that 'inner life is not rhythmic and – we can put it even more broadly – it is not lyrical. Lyrical form is introduced from outside and it expresses the axiological relationship of the other as such to the experiencing soul, and not the relationship of the experiencing soul to itself' (167). And so, in this discourse 'the outwardly solitary hero turns out not to be solitary inwardly' (Bakhtin 169). On the one hand, the lyrical work 'does not localize and does not delimit the whole of the hero totally in the outside world, and, consequently, it provides no clear-cut impression of a human being's finiteness in the world'; does not 'determine, does not delimit the movement of its hero's lived life by means of a finished and clear-cut *fabula*'; and does not 'seek to produce a finished character for the hero [...] it deals only [...] with an episode of his inner life' (Bakhtin 168). On the other, in lyric '[t]he authority of the author is the authority of a chorus. [...]; [t]his expression of value becomes strong [...] only in the chorus of others' (Bakhtin 169). Thus, Bakhtin concludes '[a] solitary and totally arbitrary breaking of silence imposes an infinite responsibility or it is cynical without justification. The voice can *sing* only in a *warm* atmosphere, only in the atmosphere of possible choral support, where *solitariness* of sound is in principle excluded' (170).

The social and cultural implications of this negation of solipsism, of the displacement in verse from authoritarian monologue to democratic dialogue, are relevant. In this regard, Raymond Williams states that the 'emergence of notions of individuality, in the modern sense, can be related to the break-up of the medieval social, economic and religious order' (163). In the movement against 'feudalism there was a new stress on a man's personal existence over and above his place or function in a rigid hierarchical society. There was a related stress, in Protestantism, on a man's direct and individual relation to God, as opposed to this relation mediated by the Church' (Williams 163-64). But it's not until the end of the seventeenth century and during the eighteenth that a 'new mode of analysis, in logic and mathematics, postulated the individual as the substantial entity [...] from which other categories and especially collective categories were derived. The political thought of the Enlightenment mainly followed this model' (Williams 164), which is at the base of modern society and culture, and which has never fully developed, it's worthwhile to clarify, in those territories occupied by colonialism, as is Cuba's case.

Williams recalls that classical economics as well as utilitarian ethics began with separate individuals who 'decided, at some starting point, to enter into economic or commercial relations' or 'calculated the consequences of this or that action which they might undertake' (164). But also in the nineteenth century began a critique of individualism that was most thoroughly expressed 'in Marx, who attacked the opposition of the abstract categories 'individual' and 'society' and argued that the individual is a social creation, born into relationships and determined by them' (164). The British theorist concludes that one ought to distinguish between individuality and individualism: 'Individuality [...] stressing both a unique person and his (indivisible) membership of a group. Individualism is a 19th century coinage [...]: a theory not only of abstract individuals but of the primacy of individual states and interest' (165). In dialogic poetry individuality is affirmed as individualism is denied, and the result is the construction of an insubordinate poetic subject, a social subject, who challenges any hierarchical, authoritarian system. And this can be applied to modern society in all its variants as much as it can be to alternatives to change it.

Dialogic poetry seeks to know reality, which it recognizes as objective existence from dissimilar philosophical positions, and yet cannot be reduced to realism.[7] A poetry that isn't assumed as a reflection but as matter, since the language that constitutes it is precisely that, and yet it cannot be reduced to instrumentalism. A poetry that is aware of its ability to intervene, to transform reality, and yet cannot be reduced to voluntarism. A poetry that critiques all oppressive and repressive power, all social hierarchy and subordination, and yet cannot be reduced to commitment. A poetry that sees itself as more than literature, drawing closer to orality, open to the most diverse languages, and yet cannot be reduced to anti-poetry. A poetry that doesn't distinguish between high and low culture, uniting with other artistic expressions, and yet cannot be reduced to populism. A poetry that seeks decolonization, in its content and form, and yet cannot be reduced to nationalism. A poetry that pursues communication through an active reader who participates just as the author does in the creation of the text, and yet cannot be reduced to didacticism. A diverse poetry, which appeals to even opposing styles, to prose and tropological density, and yet cannot be reduced to colloquialism.

III

The principle variant of dialogic poetry that has appeared in Cuba since the mid-twentieth century is colloquialism. Little has been done by traditional criticism to define this poetic trend, also called '*conversacionalismo*' both by those who affirm it and those who reject it. Virgilio López Lemus points out that it is not imported, not even from Spanish America, 'but rather has its roots, history, development and continuity' in the country itself (12). For him, Poveda, Tallet, Loynaz, Florit, Guillén, Piñera, and Feijóo, among other Cuban poets, are forerunners of the movement. Colloquialism can be characterized when verse is attentive to 'the most immediate sensations of existence' (López Lemus 11); when 'a lyrical current with epic elements' is cultivated, 'which is informed by intimism as much as it is by social poetry' (López Lemus 12); when a poetry is created that is 'nonconformist, rebellious in both form and content, full of 'anti-poetic vocabulary,' when what is used is 'prose, sarcasm, 'common' themes, that probably should be understood as quotidian, with a more informal language than the poetry that comes before it' (López Lemus 14). Ultimately, the main idea of colloquialism is a 'pronounced interest in ironizing, disdain for the bourgeois;' a 'deep, essential arriving at the popular,' where 'poets become aware of their social role' (López Lemus 16).

Colloquialism is something more than a reaction to *Orígenes*, and in particular the hermeticism of Lezama Lima and other authors in his circle, as López Lemus indicates. In that regard, he recalls that the first anti-*origenista* declarations come from 'some of the poets from the same generation as the group, and others who came immediately before.' Later, there are those from 'within the group itself, when [in 1955 the journal] *Ciclón* appears and expresses views [...] that tend to break with hermeticism' (24). Furthermore, 'colloquialists who first ascribe to *origenismo* are reacting at the same time to a kind of intimism cultivated by the generation before *Orígenes* [...] and to a neo-romantic trend, which develops 'powerful' tentacles in the fifties' (López Lemus 24). In sum, for the colloquial poets who emerge during that decade and who reach maturity during the

Revolution 'their respective paths in the new social conditions on the island are not those of the *origenistas* [...] or the neo-romantics [...], or the more introspective or religiously-inclined intimists' (López Lemus 27). In fact, these poets are going to launch, significantly, 'an offensive against what some call populism' (López Lemus 41), a trend that will unfortunately be resurrected in the seventies.

In general, for López Lemus, colloquial poetry 'starts with conversation, using the more poetic devices of *dialogue*, though it is mostly monologic; its interlocutor can be a reader or a listener the poetic voice addresses, who can appear using other grammatical persons for the lyrical subject (we, he, them...)' (11). The critic clarifies that here 'what's overcome is the resistance of natural language to transform it into artistic language. Thus, the conversational tone, which is nothing new in poetry, isn't exactly a way of conversing' (12). Still in the case of a precursor to colloquialism like Nicolás Guillén's *Elegía a Jesús Mendéndez* (1951), López Lemus keenly notes that along with the 'conversational tone,' others elements are incorporated such as 'newspaper quotes, statistics, company names, initials, words from other languages, especially taken from capitalist jargon' (22). Beyond this expansion of lexicon, there is 'free verse, prose, metre (mostly abandoned by colloquialists though used by some poets along with free verse), lyricism and epic, poetry of combat, of denouncement, of witness, and historical elements' (López Lemus 22).

In their relevant study of contemporary Latin American poetry, Mike González and David Treece present a characterization of the poetry of Salvadoran Roque Dalton that can be applied to the dialogic poetry written in Cuba during the Revolution:

> [it] addresses two different traditions: the petty bourgeois individualism of the lyric poet, and the rigidities of Stalinism. What they have in common is their exclusion from the process of creative transformation. What is called 'conversational poetry' – though the concept of 'democratic' poetry seems preferable – locates the collective at the heart of poetic language. This means recuperating the traditions of popular

culture, the patterns and rhythms of speech, the alternative history told in the oral myth, and molding the redemptive revolutionary vision out of material of everyday life. The process is not reductive, but expansive. (305)

The indisputable quality of the poetry by Jorge Enrique Adoum, Enrique Lihn, Juan Gelman, Juan Calzadilla, José Emilio Pacheco, and Antonio Cisneros undoubtedly proves it.

For Saúl Yurkievich, the dialogic poets who emerge in Latin America beginning in the fifties, and who are linked with both colloquialists and other Cuban dialogic poets of the moment, want 'to bring together progressive ideology and formal breadth' (153). At the same time they are 'formalists' and 'realists', and set out to insert their writing 'in contemporary reality [...] as a process of material production, and not as a [...] transcendental trampoline, not as an aphrodisiac or hallucinogen' (Yurkievich 153). They react against the 'illusive naturalness and intellectual impoverishment of populist intellectualism' (Yurkievich 153). Thus, 'undogmatic, uncensoring, asymmetrical,' these poets strive 'to say all that is sayable, without alienating the poetic sign's specific necessities, knowing above all that it is a verbal occurrence subject to its own processes,' which they aimed 'to exploit and advance.' Theirs is a 'multipurpose, multiphonic, multivoiced poetics,' seeking 'to unite the cutting edge of both politics and art in one common cause' (Yurkievich 153). Ultimately, poetry stops being monologic to become dialogic, to create a tapestry of socially and culturally inclusive voices, a greater democracy in representation.

IV

The Cuban poets who write dialogic poetry have faced, in the second half of the twentieth century, a favourable social-cultural reality only in appearances. In other words, if in theory a process of decolonization like the one carried out in Cuba encourages writing of that nature, in practice it has been severely limited. At the base of this contradiction is the fact that intellectuals have not had a prominent role in the Cuban Revolution. As Roberto

Fernández Retamar reveals, during the assault on the Moncada Barracks in Santiago de Cuba in 1953, and then later during the insurrectional phase in 1956, which would lead to the overthrow in 1959, 'the participation of intellectuals who were contemporaries of the political leaders, was infrequent' (271-272). And it will continue to be despite enthusiastically joining up with the Revolution's triumph and process, leaving behind 'political despondency and detachment that had been exalted by the most visible part of the previous generation [*Orígenes*]' and that had initially caught on with the young poets, along with the 'voluntary exile that would take them to New York, Paris, Madrid, and Rome. Obviously, these were poets of a bourgeois or petite bourgeois background' (Fernández Retamar 272).

And, in more than half a century of Cuban Revolution, not only has a true dialogue between political leaders and intellectuals been missing, the former has only given the latter a very limited space for integration, which has only rarely surpassed the boundaries of cultural activity. In the 1966 essay cited above, Fernández Retamar proposes, 'Cuban intellectuals, who have lucidly debated aesthetic questions, should consider other aspects, under penalty of staying confined to the limits of their guild' (281).Unfortunately, this is where it has remained to the present day, and scarcely a handful of them – in the case of the poets selected here, only Fernández Retamar himself along with Miguel Barnet – have had access to the maximum institutions of power, and then more as representatives of a social sector than with any true capacity to make decisions. As Desiderio Navarro states, the revolutionary leaders have perceived intellectuals, at every moment, as 'untrustworthy companions, and even a potential oppositional political force' (694), and have allowed for the propagation of 'anti-intellectualism, already existent in Cuban culture, but heightened and disseminated for political ends' (703).

Navarro recalls that in 1961 Fidel Castro came up with a phrase that has been the cornerstone of the island's cultural politics since that time: 'Within the Revolution everything; against the Revolution nothing'. Removed from its context and in the hands of all kinds of circumstantial hermeneuts and exegetes, this line [...] would illustrate an extraordinary polysemy, which would allow it to be the guiding principle recognized by successive periods and trends at work' (690). If for the majority of the revolutionary intellectuals it was clear their social role ought to be critical, it was not so for the majority of the political leaders. And beginning in 1968

> a true crusade against intellectual critical intervention in the public sphere came about, a crusade that culminated in the First National Conference on Education and Culture (1971) and only came apart at the beginning of the eighties with the last failed attempt to implant Soviet Socialist Realism in its most hostile, anti-social criticism version, as official doctrine. (Navarro 694)

At the beginning of the eighties 'once again critical voices are heard, this time with greater force and numbers, belonging to young intellectuals born with and educated by the Revolution' (Navarro 694). The majority this time came from the working class and the peasantry.[8] In this way, what Ernesto Che Guevara proposes in 'Socialism and Man in Cuba' against Socialist Realism and in favor of the intellectual's critical position is revitalized.[9] This willingness for public discussion produced 'an unheard of proliferation of all kinds of cultural spaces: exhibition, publication, reading spaces [...]; institutional and non-institutional spaces; private and public spaces' (Navarro 695). Yet 'the new critical interventions and spaces of the eighties were erased in the nineties. The modus operandi ranged from crass removal from dictionaries and historical texts to the subtle and immediate acceptance [...] of the euphemism 'grey five years' (1971-1975) for the period of authoritarianism and dogmatism that, on the one hand lasted [...] approximately from 1968 to 1983, and on the other, was black for many lives and quite a lot of artistic output' (Navarro 702-703).

From its beginnings to the present day, in the complex process of the Cuban Revolution, 'the role of the revolutionary intellectual as critical of revolutionary social reality is rarely denied openly, yet it is also rarely affirmed or reaffirmed straight out; most of the time it is silenced or mentioned in passing as merely an minor or optional feature' (Navarro 697). In fact, 'at the heart of Cuban socialism what is expected of Marxist criticism [...] is that social aspects of artistic communication are studied in a less sociological way, in other words, *that it be less Marxist or even not Marxist at all*' (Navarro 699). These successive offenses by Cuban revolutionary power against the critical interventions of intellectuals in the public sphere have ultimately generated pessimism, disillusionment, scepticism, resentment, which along with the difficult work and living conditions caused by the crisis in the nineties, has led to 'the scattering of the majority of the artistic intelligentsia throughout the Americas and Europe' (Navarro 696).

V

When taking stock of poetry's first moment in the Revolution, which extends from 1959 to 1971, Vitier points out that this process 'with regard to a taking over of our historical and cultural beings, made it possible for Cuban poetry to grow closer chorally to concrete events, immediate realities, stripped of compensatory or prophetic images, without mythical nostalgia or Tantalus's thirst. This opportunity was taken advantage of with the greatest diligence and good results' (Raúl 5). That participative verse, as Fernández Retamar and Jamís, editors of the anthology *Poesía joven de Cuba* [Young Cuban Poetry] (Havana: II Festival del Libro Cubano, 1959) made very clear, set out 'to insist on [its] diversity,' and was characterized by 'a direct, conversational tone, which in some [of the selected poets] had existed before 1959' (quoted in López Lemus 55-56). At its centre, as Arturo Arango suggests, was the reconsideration of the relationships 'between poetry and ideology, between poetry and politics, [...] between poetry and its recipients' (Para llegar 12). Social changes had intensified in these poets 'the need to incorporate others areas of reality, to adopt as their own the impurities of the common man's language [...]. Indeed, the need for rupture was accentuated [...]. The changes in poetics [...] appeared now as part of a natural, periodical, and above all, *revolutionary* process (Arango Para llegar 12-13).

What then unfolds is a period of splendour for Cuban poetry, where older avant-garde and *origenista* poets participate, but where the young ones, who opt for colloquialism and other variants of dialogic poetry stand out. As one of its most severe critics, Jorge Luis Arcos, recognizes, colloquialism 'showed revolutionary transformations in reality, created a deeper awareness of the interdependence between poets and their circumstances, and witnessed man's dramatic conflicts to transform himself and his context, and it accomplished a deep critique of the past, projections that have deeply marked the poetic consciousness of the nation (Introducción xxxvi-xxxvii). This poetry too 'was certainly able to express a different world view' and 'positioned itself within the expression of the immanent world, which it tried to provide with a new transcendence. Of course, this wasn't always achieved;' and a 'legitimate idealism' for seeking 'reality's transformation was upheld.' On the other hand, its 'lexical and stylistic openness, in general, broadened poetry's cognitive capacity to express new facets of reality' (Arcos Introducción xxxvii).

The first reaction against colloquialism comes from the poets who gather around the publisher Ediciones El Puente [The Bridge] (1961-1965), who are considered the first of a new generation. The very name of the group 'testifies to the self-awareness of the precarious place where history situated them' (Arango Para llegar 16). They propose a poetry of 'intimacy, being, where revolutionary context, history, are mostly in the background, preferring to be contemplative: to be simply, no emphasis, no ideological declamations' (Arango Para llegar 16). In the El Puente group there is a notable presence of poets from the popular classes, women, Afro-Cubans, and homosexuals. The group organized around the journal *El Caimán Barbudo*, which in 1966 'would come to be the forum of young Cuban poetry, was basically white, male, and heterosexual' (Arango Para llegar 17). The latter will present themselves, in the cultural magazine's first issue, with the polemical manifesto 'Nos pronunciamos' [We Declare Ourselves]. Undoubtedly, in both cases this generation wants to distinguish itself from the previous, and is mostly inclined toward an anti-poetic, prose-like colloquialism.[10]

Yet, 'Nos pronunciamos' is a radical manifesto of dialogic poetry that goes beyond colloquialism.[11] Above all it affirms a critical will, since it didn't propose to 'write poetry to the Revolution' but 'from and because of the Revolution. Revolutionary literature cannot be apologetic' (quoted in García Sánchez 9-10). It expresses a willingness to represent reality in all its vastness and profundity, to go beyond the barriers between public and private. It does not renounce 'so-called unsocial topics. Love and conflict with death, are circumstances that affect us all, just as authentic revolutionary commitment is intimate, personal' (quoted in García Sánchez 9-10). Ultimately, they believed 'every subject is fit for poetry' (quoted in García Sánchez 9-10). At the same time, they reject poetry 'that attempts to justify itself with revolutionary denotations, repetitions of poor, overused formulas,' like 'trying to hide behind 'poetic' words, charged with cheap metaphysics to place man outside of his circumstances' (quoted in García Sánchez 9-10). What is significant is their emphasis on the democratization of language and their approach to popular culture, since they seek 'the integration of Cuban speech into poetry' and consider that 'in the texts of our popular, folk music there are poetic possibilities' (quoted in García Sánchez 9-10).

Still the evolution of colloquialism and all kinds of dialogic poetry in Cuba was cut short beginning in 1968 – and even more so, in 1971– with revolutionary power's offensive against the critical intervention of intellectuals in the public sphere. The establishing of colloquialism as the dominant trend in Cuban poetry in the sixties is a natural process with roots in Cuban literature itself. The new poetic norm, a barely tropicalized Socialist Realism, turns out to be an artificial imposition, lacking any real tradition in the island's literary output. On the one hand, the majority of the leading voices of the era's dialogic poetry from both the established generation and the emerging one are silenced. In its place what is encouraged is poetry to the Revolution written by hired hands compliant with official thought.[12] Not only is a critical will rejected, but also any formal boldness, and clarity is emphasized, which ultimately pre-supposes a passive reader. In essence, it is monologic poetry, in content and form, a false *conversacionalismo*, which, even 'proposed to purge poetry of prosaicism and other colloquial excesses' (Arango Para llegar 21).

VI

Poetry – and at its heart, dialogic poetry – shines once more in Cuba at the beginning of the eighties, and this wealth extends to the end of the century. A new poetics is established then, which, as Vitier himself notes, approaches the work of *Orígenes*, but on its own terms. It is a

> new invention of reality in a different context, with a different meaning. It is no longer about experiencing the impossible as an existential quality linked to (not exhausted by) historical frustration, but rather a rediscovering [...] of the eternal themes of man in the area of the unknown. There is practically no more profound proof of the spiritual authenticity of our Revolution, than it becoming, from the viewpoint of dreams, a sure foundation for the reconsideration of fable and symbol. (*Enigma* 5)

Within the diversity that makes the end of official and unofficial promotion of Socialist Realism possible, a gradual, healthy displacement of colloquialism to other aspects of dialogic poetry occurs.[13]

In this renaissance participate at least three groups of poets: *Orígenes*, the Fifties Generation, and the El Puente-*El Caimán Barbudo* Generation, and especially their silenced authors, who begin to publish once more. Additionally, there is a formidable growth of the poetry from the diaspora.[14] A new generation of poets is also incorporated, which, depending on how one defines these divisions, could be considered part of the last generation mentioned or a new one. More important is to recognize, as León de la Hoz does, that what marks this new group is 'nonconformity with all that's been poorly done and those who are responsible for it' (37). These young poets confront 'the trivialization of ideology and certain outdated, supposedly unchanging values produced by the very process [...]. They oppose homogenization, control, schematics, and dogmatism, which attempt to judge them in proportion to other generations and in another context' (Hoz 37). In sum, they have been 'educated in a system that on occasion contradicts its own propositions,' and 'see in literature a transforming power and in criticism a method to oppose errors and deficiencies' (Hoz 37).

The poets who at this moment break with Socialist Realism but at the same time refuse solipsism, find in colloquialism the point of departure to develop their work. They recognize that conversational verse was 'much more than the echo of an official discourse' (Arango Para llegar 29), or in other words, a moral and aesthetically legitimate poetics. For this reason they move on to critical appropriation, to the negation of the negation, to emphasize continuity over rupture, as *Usted es la culpable: Nueva poesía cubana* (Víctor Rodríguez Núñez, editor, Havana, Editora Abril, 1985) attests. This poetry, as de la Hoz points out, deals with topics 'of an ontological character' (35), and its 'analytical poetic subject' achieves an 'ethical problematization of the individual within the revolutionary process and its social body' (41). The poetic subjects are 'open, true to themselves, anxious to express all their individual dimensions, against norms and prejudices' (Hoz 37). Among other achievements, this poetry produces 'texts with a strong homosexual content and feminine recognition' (Hoz 41). A highlight is that there is not just one 'centre, but a movement throughout the country' (Hoz 42).

The distancing from colloquialism, in the work by this new generation, will become more accentuated and beneficial. A concern for reflection, as de la Hoz sustains, makes poetic expression 'sententious or verse expands, or rhythm turns melodious. There is the desire to transmit ideas and beautify expression by dissociating from earlier models of representation. Poets do so by using more allegorization, symbolization and invention' (42). Critical intentions are projected in some cases through 'irony, prose, impudence, and intertexuality' (Hoz 42). Ultimately, 'a dominant language doesn't exist, but rather a growing experimentation with a marked eagerness for authenticity [...]: tropological cathedrals, pomposity and simplicity, verse, euphony and noise, confidence and ease' (Hoz 41). And yet it doesn't renounce the dialogic condition; it reconsiders

> the relationship work-reader. There's a willingness to communicate with the advantages of conversational language [...]. Though direct contact through public readings is not abandoned, what's preferred is a confidential relationship with the reader and the printed word. Discourse becomes polysemic, suggestive, fragmented, and connotative; so the reader is called to participate actively and creatively and the relationship has multiple meanings. (Hoz 41-42)

By the end of the eighties, Cuban poetry is transformed by the advent of another new generation, which is presented in the anthology *Retrato de grupo* (Havana: Letras Cubanas, 1989). In its pages, according to Arango, 'there is a different conception of poetry, and its relationship to ideology and history' (Para llegar 28). In fact, the refusal by the editors – Carlos Augusto Alfonso, Víctor Fowler, Emilio García Montiel, and Antonio José Ponte – to formulate some kind of unifying project demonstrates 'their decentering, their choosing marginality, their own dispersion' (Arango Para llegar 28). Furthermore, 'a diversity that is one of its principal assets' (Arango Para llegar 29) manifests itself in content and form. What is produced is '[a]transition that perhaps once more comes from history and where poetry intervenes as a response to the perplexities the present imposes' (Arango Para llegar 27).[15] Yet not even the most extreme reaction to colloquialism, the neo-baroque, with its relative hermeticism, implies a return to solipsism, since it stresses an active, participative reader.

VII

This anthology, edited and translated by Katherine M. Hedeen, proposes to be the continuation of *Cincuenta años de poesía cubana*, the 1952 survey in which Vitier was able 'to demonstrate within a range of respectable breadth and minimal rigor, what has been and is our Republic's poetry' (Introducción 5). Accordingly, the present selection begins where its predecessor left off, but without excluding the new poets who appeared there, who later created notable work. In other words, here are present not only the majority of authors from the chapter 'Poetas de aparición más reciente' – Carilda Oliver Labra, Jamís, and Fernández Retamar, among others – but also the two youngest figures among 'Los poetas de *Orígenes*' – Fina García-Marruz and Lorenzo García Vega, who've opened up new avenues in the island's poetry. In this retrospective, although the generational method is ruled out, Hedeen has sought a fitting representation of each group. Furthermore, historical order prevails over logical classification, since authors and their work take place in a specific context. Yet, the poetic process is presented not as a lineal progression but with its contradictory character, with its thesis, antithesis, and synthesis.

The anthology's intention is to offer a representative sample of dialogic poetry written in Cuba from 1952 to 2000. It gives voice to all its fundamental constructions, without stressing one subject specifically, and much less the construction of the Cuban nation. Nationalism is always exclusive and discriminatory, the most harmful ideology of modern society, the mistaken path toward decolonization. There is no appeal to the system of social quotas or the balance between writing on and off the island, but to the worth of poetry itself, as well as the faithfulness of the authors to this kind of writing. It has tried to avoid, with particular care, 'exogenous yet very real polarization, false yet impoverished reception,' which José Prats Sariol warns us of, and which has its base in political positioning (10). It doesn't attempt to be outside the game of politics – a dangerous illusion – but recognizes the relative independence of poetry. This has not impeded but facilitated the documenting, in the case of Cuba during this moment, of poetic subjects who challenge all social oppression and repression.

Indispensable for Hedeen in the carrying out of this anthology have been the books that precede it, like *Las palabras son islas: Panorama de la poesía cubana del siglo XX* (Havana: Letras Cubanas, 1991), by Arcos; *Poesía cubana del siglo XX: Antología* (Mexico: FCE, 2002), by Jesús J. Barquet and Norberto Codina; and *Antología de la poesía cubana, Tomo IV, Siglo XX* (Madrid: Verbum, 2002), by Ángel Esteban and Álvaro Salvador. In addition, other selections of specific moments of the process like *La Generación de los años 50: Antología poética* (Havana: Letras Cubanas, 1984), by Luis Suardíaz, David Chericián, and Eduardo López Morales; *Los ríos de la mañana: Poesía cubana de los 80* (Havana: Unión, 1995), by Arturo Arango and Codina; and *Poesía cubana: La isla entera* (Madrid: Betania, 1995) by Felipe Lázaro and Bladimir Zamora. My own anthologies have informed this work as well.[16] An extensive bibliography on the field of study has been widely consulted.

Hedeen has not established hierarchies of any kind among the poets here. In this way, all the poets chosen have more or less the same amount of pages, enough to have a fair vision of their work. As for the notes, she has tried to offer pertinent biographical information, as well as a bibliography for each, though only poetry books are considered. At every moment there is a balance in handling this material, between a poetic perception and an academic one. In this way, beauty and utility come together. What cannot be denied in these pages is the quality of the poetry presented, one of the best the Spanish language offers in the twentieth century.

Víctor Rodríguez Núñez
Havana-Gambier-Paris, May-August 2011-Gambier, May 2015

Notes

[1] Translations of Vitier, López Lemus, Yurkievich, Fernández Retamar, Navarro, Silva León, García Sánchez, Arango, Rodríguez Rivera, Espinosa Domínguez, and de la Hoz are the responsibility of the translator.

[2] *Modernismo* refers to the influential Spanish American literary movement of the late nineteenth and early twentieth centuries. It stems from a reaction against literary naturalism and bourgeois conformity and materialism. In general terms, it is characterized by innovation of literary form and an openness to diverse, 'exotic' cultures.

[3] I broach the latter topic in my essay 'La in/subordinación intelectual en *Bustos y rimas*, de Julián del Casal'. *Revista de Estudios Hispánicos* 42-1 (January 2008): 51-81.

4. It should be noted that this does not hinder her from constructing a poetic subject who challenges the patriarchal norm in her collection *Versos* (1938). See my article: 'La in/subordinación de género en *Versos* de Dulce María Loynaz'. *Revista de Estudios Hispánicos* 35-2 (May 2001): 389-418.

5. Ballagas will construct a subject who challenges the heterosexual norm in *Cielo en rehenes* (1951). Refer to my essay: 'El cielo del rehén: La in/subordinación sexual en los versos tardíos de Emilio Ballagas'. *Revista de Crítica Literaria Latinoamericana* 55 (2002): 133-56.

6. See my article: '*Extrañeza de estar*, certidumbre del otro: La poesía temprana de Cintio Vitier'. *Hispamérica* 84 (1999): 23-35.

7. Terry Eagleton recalls that it was the Russian Formalists who first questioned the revolutionary character of Realism, a critical position that will later become the cornerstone of Bertolt Brecht's theater and Roland Barthes' literary theory. According to Barthes, Realism 'tends to conceal the socially relative or constructed nature of language: it helps to confirm the prejudice that there is a form of 'ordinary' language which is somehow natural. This natural language gives us reality 'as it is': it does not – like Romanticism or Symbolism – distort it into subjective shapes, but represents the world to us as God himself might know it' (Eagleton 117). As for Brecht, he uses 'the so-called 'estrangement effect' to render the most taken-for-granted aspects of social reality shockingly unfamiliar, and so to rouse the audience to a new critical awareness of them. Far from being concerned to reinforce the audience's sense of security, Brecht wants, as he says, to 'create contradictions within them' – to unsettle their convictions, dismantle and refashion their received identities, and expose the unity of this selfhood as an ideological illusion' (Eagleton 162).

8. As Louis A. Pérez, Jr. notes: 'the most notable achievements of the [R]evolution occurred in the areas of education, nutrition, and health services. Indeed, nowhere was the quest for an egalitarian society more fully attained than in the area of education. No longer was education restricted to Cubans of means, no longer was the opportunity for education confined to Cubans in urban areas' (272-273). In 1962, 'the revolutionary government reported the adult literacy rate to be 96 percent, the highest in Latin America and one of the highest in the world' (Pérez 273). Arnaldo Silva León offers these numbers: '[f]rom 811,345 students enrolled in the education system in 1958, in 1975 there were 3,051,060. In that same period,

elementary education increased 2.7 times; middle school education by 6.1 [...]. In 1975, rates of schooling for children between the ages of six and twelve was one hundred percent. The number of scholarship students was 600,000 between boarders and semi-boarders. [...] From less than 30,000 graduates of sixth grade in 1958, the number rose to nearly 190,000 in 1975' (267). The Revolution also transformed 'the character and content of higher education. The number of university centers increased from three in 1959 to forty in the 1980s; enrollments expanded tenfold' (Pérez 274). The growth in education opened new horizons for literature: '[i]n 1962, the National Publisher of Cuba was created, and in 1967, the Cuban Book Institute. In 1958, the country produced approximately a million books. In 1967, this number rose to eight million, and in 1975, 35 million' (Silva León 268). In 1985, 'the country had 319 public libraries and 3,200 scholarly ones. In the five years spanning 1981-1985, more than 5,000 different titles were brought out, with an annual book production of 40 million' (Silva León 299-300).

[9] Guevara says the following about Socialist Realism: 'We revolutionaries often lack the knowledge and intellectual audacity needed to meet the task of developing the new man and woman with methods different from the conventional ones [...]. What is sought then is simplification, something everyone can understand, something functionaries understand. True artistic experimentation ends, and the problem of general culture is reduced to assimilating the socialist present and the dead (therefore, not dangerous) past. [...] The realistic art of the 19th century, however, also has a class character, more purely capitalist perhaps than the decadent art of the 20th century that reveals the anguish of the alienated individual. [...] But why try to find the only valid prescription in the frozen forms of Socialist Realism?' (www.marxists.org). Guevara also recognizes the critical role of intellectuals: 'We must not create either docile servants of official thought, or 'scholarship students' who live at the expense of the state – practicing freedom in quotation marks' (www.marxist.org).

[10] In 1966, according to Fernández Retamar, '[i]n Cuba there are three visible generations [...].' These generations are the ''avant-garde generation' [...]; the 'between revolutions generation,' which comes of age between the failed 1933 revolution and the current Revolution's access to power, in 1959; and lastly the 'first generation of the Revolution,' which comes about in that process. The earliest of those who are emerging now ('second generation of the

Revolution') coincide in quite a few areas with this latter generation' (266-267).

[11] It's worthwhile clarifying that this was not the intention of the poets who signed the manifesto. Guillermo Rodríguez Rivera characterizes the poetry of this generation as the 'establishing of a new prose poetry that takes advantage of the expressive conquests of the avant-garde' (5). He adds, '[i]f post-*modernismo* prosaicism appears as a hiatus between *modernismo* and the powerful avant-garde that will emerge in the century's third decade; if until then prose poetry was seen as only a minor trend, always in the background, behind the dominant poetry of unusual images, this relationship will change, and it seems to me to be irrefutable that, beginning in the forties, this trend will slowly begin to impose itself at the center of the work by poets from various generations [...] and as a principal force of poetry in Spanish' (6).

[12] This generation, as opposed to all the others from the second half of the twentieth century, has no anthology to define it. Arango has referred to 'the strange, little studied evolution' of this generation, 'which emerged after the first five years of the Revolution, assuming it in an integral, participative way, and has suffered like none other the traumas of the political (as well as ideological and aesthetic) contradictions of a process with the intensity, dimension, and complexities like ours' (Años 203-204). The critic adds, 'if in 1959 poets celebrated the reconciliation of poetry with history, the *El Caimán* Generation had to live a new rupture. The Cuban Revolution, which had been characterized in its first decade for offering spaces up until that point unknown for intellectual labor, for practicing thought and art as a whole, began the seventies submerged in a crisis that would lead to strong dogmatization. As is well-known, for ideological and political reasons, the majority of active poets were excluded from publishers' catalogs and from the pages of up until then flourishing cultural journals. The *El Caimán* Generation was paralyzed by this period of dogmatizations. Their exclusion wasn't limited to names; but also as could be expected, in the very utterance of a new motto. The official slogan was: 'Art is a weapon of the Revolution,' which not only excluded whatever was against the process, but also whatever wasn't, whatever managed to do without politics or ideology' (Para llegar 20-21).

[13] For an account of the opposition of intellectuals to Socialist Realism, see: Arango, Arturo. 'Historia de otra pelea cubana contra los

demonios'. *Segundas reincidencias*. Santa Clara: Editorial Capiro, 2002. 51-60.

[14] For Carlos Espinosa Domínguez, the seventies constitute, for the literature of the Cuban diaspora, 'its moment of takeoff,' since 'quality and formal concerns will prevail over anti-Castro cries and hasty condemnations' (12). The eighties become its 'definitive consolidation,' in which there is 'a progressive, prominent rise in poetry production' (Espinosa Domínguez 16). Espinosa Domínguez adds, '[i]n the varied scale of orientations and styles that Cuban poetry of exile has offered in the last two decades, what has stood out is the return to classical metre, the recognition and acknowledgement of the legacy of *Orígenes*, the advancement of colloquialism and poetry of experience, the resurgence of a new social poetry, now without having to serve politics, and a writing where a subtle feminine gaze is important, which makes itself evident not only through a certain kind of expression of feeling, but also in language and the selection of subject matter' (17). In the anthology *Cuban American Writers: Los Atrevidos* (1988), for the first time, 'Cuban literature of the diaspora finds its true connections with the rest of the Hispanic authors in the United States' (Espinosa Domínguez 21).

[15] As Louis A. Pérez, Jr. reveals, the so-called Special Period – which begins in Cuba in 1991, with the disintegration of the USSR and the Socialist camp and continues on into the present – has been a true trauma 'experienced variously by hundreds of thousands of households across the island as scarcity, want, and hunger [...]. The período especial affected more than the patterns of daily life. Changed too were the ways that Cubans took measure of their circumstances. Not perhaps since the 1960s were existing value systems subject to as much pressure as they were during the 1990s. Much of this had to do with morality after belief had failed. New fault lines appeared on the moral topography of Cuban daily life and acted to reconfigure the normative terms by which Cuban entered the twenty-first century. The período especial must be seen as a defining experience, although the direction and the distance – perhaps the depth – of the new fault lines are not yet apparent. An entire generation came of age during those years, and it remains to be seen how the experience will act to shape the future of Cuba' (298).

[16] See: *Cuba: En su lugar la poesía* (in collaboration with Reina María Rodríguez and Osvaldo Sánchez; Mexico: U Autónoma Metropol-

itana-Azcapotzalco, 1982); the previously mentioned *Usted es la culpable: Nueva poesía cubana*; and *El pasado del cielo: La nueva y novísima poesía cubana* (Medellin: Alejandría Editores, 1994).

Works Cited

Arcos, Jorge Luis. 'Introducción a la poesía cubana del siglo XX'. *Las palabras son islas: Panorama de la poesía cubana del siglo XX (1900-1998)*. Ed. Arcos. Havana: Letras Cubanas, 1999. xix-xliii.

Arango, Arturo. 'Con los años a favor'. *Antología boreal*. By Lina de Feria. Havana: Letras Cubanas, 2007. 202-4.

— 'Para llegar a la poesía cubana de hoy'. *Cuadernos Hispano-americanos* 706 (April 2009): 7-33.

Bakhtin, M.M. *Art and Answerability: Early Philosophical Essays*. Eds. Michael Holquist and Vadim Liapunov. Trans. Vadim Liapunov. Austin: U of Texas P, 1990.

Eagleton, Terry. *Literary Theory: An Introduction*. 2nd Edition. Minneapolis: U of Minnesota P. 1998.

Espinosa Domínguez, Carlos. 'Introducción'. *La pérdida y el sueño: Antología de poetas cubanos en la Florida*. Ed. Espinosa Domínguez. Cincinnati: Término Editorial, 2001. 9-26.

Fernández Retamar, Roberto. 'Hacia una intelectualidad revolucionaria en Cuba'. *Cuba defendida*. Havana: Letras Cubanas, 2004. 265-290.

García Sánchez, Jesús. 'Prólogo'. *Hay muchos modos de jugar: Antología poética*. Madrid: Visor, n/d. 7-22.

González, Mike and David Treece. *The Gathering of Voices: The Twentieth Century Poetry of Latin America*. New York: Verso, 1992.

Guevara, Ernesto Che. *Socialism and Man in Cuba*. Trans. Brian Baggins. Ocean Press, 2005. North Melborne: Ocean Press. https://www.marxists.org/archive/guevara/1965/03/man-socialism.htm

Hoz, León de la 'Generaciones, degeneraciones, regeneraciones'. *La poesía de las dos orillas: Cuba (1959-1993)*. Ed. de la Hoz. Madrid: Libertarias/Prodhufi, 1994. 11-61.

López Lemus, Virgilio. *Palabras del trasfondo*. Havana: Letras Cubanas, 1988.

Navarro, Desiderio. 'In medias res publicas: Sobre los intelectuales y la crítica social en la esfera pública cubana'. *Ensayo cubano del siglo XX*. Ed. and intro. Rafael Hernández and Rafael Rojas. Mexico: FCE, 2002. 689-707.

Pérez, Jr. Louis A. *Cuba: Between Reform and Revolution*. Third Edition. New York: Oxford UP, 2006.

Silva León, Arnaldo. 'La Revolución en el poder (1959-1995)'. *Cuba y su historia*. by Francisca Lópeza Civeira, Oscar Loyola Vega, and Silva León. Havana: Gente Nueva, 1998.

Yurkievich, Saúl. *La confabulación con la palabra*. Madrid: Taurus, 1978.

Vitier, Cintio. 'Introducción'. *Cincuenta años de poesía cubana, 1902-1952*. Ed. Vitier. Havana: Dirección de Cultura del Ministerio de Educación, 1952. 1-7.

— 'Prólogo'. *Enigma de la saguas*. By Raúl Hernández Novás. Havana: Universidad de La Habana, 1983. 5-8.

— 'Solipsismo y Revolución (A propósito de *Con figura de gente y en uso de razón*, de Francisco de Oraá)'. *Obras 4: Crítica 2*. Havana: Letras Cubanas, 2001. 291-94.

Williams, Raymond. *Keywords: A Vocabulary of Culture and Society*. New York: Oxford UP, 1983.

Fina García-Marruz

There's No Time to Start from the Beginning...

Long live my body dark and restless
       Martí

There's no time to start from the beginning, everything
in order, shamelessly, in the elemental, candid blue.
There's no possible lucidity, the circle's closed off
its horizon where humble paradises swaggered.
There's no time now to be, in some way, distinguished
like a donkey, a grapevine, and to the same end
there's no time to ignore it all completely.
And now is the time for smiling like fools
watching child's play and youth's fury,
and thinking it's understood, content with the small birds
that storm, legs unmoving, in leaps, two by two.
Still the future will always shine ancient before diminutive present,
before daily possession, blinding privilege.
There's no time now for innocence and individual face.
Misfortune corrupting us, changes our names on a whim.
And while we begin to look like everyone in life and death,
in sin and desire, in undoing and night,
unnerved we enter what's uniform, and then,
like a wild promise, we feel in our shoulders
the unmerited investiture of what's living, what's dark.

1955

Our Indians

> *today they wander like fairies*
> *beneath the moon's splendour*
> Plácido

They did not leave us imposing temples
where stone howled
with the imagination of serpent,
flower, thunder, or waters.
No mysterious syllables
atl, tla, 'I suffer,' 'water,'
to remind us of suffering by water,
Atlantic sinking, the flood
told by the ancient chronicles,
whose trace remains in those faces,
age-old, mute,
scored in the obsidian,
taking us back to Henoch, the name of Noah
in reverse, and to Tenochtitlán, rich
with markets and plazas.

They did not leave us that swishing language
where consonants whistled like birds
in a muddleheaded glen, or like arrows
so swift, feathered blowguns
flying toward the branchy arches
where the boy actor descended crossing
dressed like a butterfly.
Only some names
where the o or the a opened and closed
twilights and dawns: a always maternal,
aquatic always, n's as in canoe,
o's as in overheard, conch, or caracole,
cao, coa, aca, so began
many of those words
from their tenderly vocalic tongue,
since it's the vowels that sing,
that let light into name.

Humble stones they left us,
no arrogant stones.
Hammock, ball, casabe,
happiness found in rest,
play in light,
wisdom of bread.
Mild they were and 'gentle and always laughing.'
Their epitaph the flower's: I left no traces.
What traces does the day leave,
the fine morning, with scenes
of fishing or bathing,
what trace love's quick glance?

What true
greatness, whether solemn or amusing,
has left more traces
than the night
or the bird in flight toward its other home?

They left no countless materials
for erudition: only a clay pot's
edge, an adornment, a bead.
Where those light movements
of graceful neck when chasing the ball
through the blue? Powerful irons
could not capture them:
Let us give thanks

They were
           like that tiny little fish
uncatchable in the net.
This is told by the Father de las Casas
who witnessed this lone areito
to have been told,
and how with music and dance
they imitated the movements of fish
at the moment of escape, escape from the strange
besieging, toward the wavy blue,
their kingdom, ours, the one untouchable eternal,
leaving, for every chronicle, this beloved story.

The Solemn Lessons

1

*...he was like the raintree
of the plains, in his splendour and generosity,
and like the rivers that fall tormented
from the peaks, and like the pinnacles
that come burning, with light and clamour,
from the insides of the earth*
      Martí's speech in honour of Bolívar

It is not in the books on rhetoric, revolution
where I find the images that might explain you,
but drawing closer to the formation of the currents,
to the fire rising from the insides of the earth
scattering heat and steam and light,
to the sea gnawing the limits of the earth
dragging along whatever it finds at its pace
to later shape new islands and continents.
It is in the elemental notions of any Physics book,
of any old Geography text for children
where you learn spirit and earth
have an air of family.
It is not in the old tropes or in the figures of speech
where you see heart connect with centre's fire,
hero with starry night,
suffering with stone,
revolution with powerful current of waters
that spring up among pinnacles like among sharp barriers
which only manage to make their current more unruly.

6

Like candlelight
from far off, seems still, never
to notice its wavering red or orange,
or like the sea's weight, where foam
frolics, bubbling, toward the crest,
or like heartbeat in tranquil breast,
life effervesces, in silence, in secret,
with another movement,
like a poet unknown by the city he sings to,
its movement is not one recognized by the crowds,
it's not the spinning star's,
or the rising or falling body's,
rather it's likened
to light waves,
invisible sound waves,
infinitesimally joyful.

Everything quivers like the plucked lute string
and the papers don't take notice.

Every beat is secret.

Carilda Oliver Labra

The Dead Neighbour Woman

The house was like her: a pale toy
clean, sad beneath the number seven.

I don't want to recall her... I'm wounded by the hem
of her white dress with an aged clasp.

There, innocently, when she'd open the door,
she was a hazy dream, an uncertain lamp:

something asking shelter from death.
Her eyes... poor eyes like a luckless flower's!

they seemed to gaze straight into me once.
She lived next to us with a fish fear.

Newlywed, alone, she washed the tablecloths
and her soul. Always faithful to her were

a bride's shyness and everlasting window.
The evening upon her was a tender tomb.

I never knew her name. I don't know it still...
But after her death I will call her María.

1951

To Hope I Return, to the Wood

To hope I return, to the wood
that built my important days,
to the wayward spring
of times past.

To the justice of seeing it all
as if it belonged to me,
for when it's said and done there's no way
to abandon the hunger of the beast.

1962

Lost Words

I don't complain of what's terrible appearing:
this tooth I've lost is one of its signs,
this deafening storm one of its traits.
There's nothing to be done,
I can't get the code right.

Now a page draws closer and takes me all at once.
It's like a sudden lover unexpected,
possessing us in the tremble of twilight
with not one careless syllable.
Under its magic I find the first woman
I surely was.
I am dead, I know,
though I stroll along Tirry Avenue
and I'm amazed by its caryatids.

I follow what doesn't exist and always know.
I sing to the storm, I am her daughter,
her forgetful one,
the last
of a race that will leave no descendants.

I catch a certain kind of meekness
when I'm granted the dew
on sea nights.

My eyes cross with the flowers I invent,
with the clouds,
nailed to this ship that took me for a castaway.

I live off a sip of rain,
off this bit of man,
and always fearful of embracing no-one.

Lorenzo García Vega

Reina Street

On the street surface the anciently intertwined. Portrait, dusty advertisements. To cross them, covering yourself with an old layer of memories. To imagine you are monstrously willing to arrive to any kind of night.

Lower back of a corner, shop window of a pharmacy. Light undone, always, on a landscape constantly reinvented. To remember at this moment that someone descended from its shoulders, to place them in the shop window, the chips, the pale chips of a game where the playing cards grew ill from the spectral tepidness of the light.

Nameless, shrill trinkets; bodegas. To understand voluptuously, in the spaciousness of an arcade, that the elegant can disguise itself with a long crown of magic knives, like a ghost made to hallucinate a foreigner. What is tattoo of a shadow like theory discarded.

The sun had no reason to set on this street. Yet it did. Of course, with such a discrete ploy that, only by spinning some arms, what it was about could be understood. Perhaps sulky, ingenuous caryatids rehearsed a vain game of repetitions.

Noise from car horns, withered lights on broken patios, small, silver hands to surprise randomly, small paintings of daubed eyes to crush incantations, crude, diminutive image of Saint Barbara. All that, in a minute, slips, spills like night's specks, stays still on the balconies.

Though we scarcely understand, to linger halfway down the block, facing a store of sacred images. To wait, tangled in the memory of the scent of a kitchen, for us to be up to learning this absurd technique now bending over the plaster backs of some hallucinatingly clumsy angels.

Dry Rain

Or, rather, it's the rain with water unwetting. Rain, the most distant rain you can imagine. Where a dream – yet is it exactly a dream? – could perhaps specify its figuration, so full of old rubble.

I'll also warn this rain shows nothing. It's already too distant, it shows nothing.

I would say it tosses and turns, diminutively, if by chance you could say something about it. But it's nothing. Nothing I can say about it. If I try to imagine it, it's as if I tried to fix an empty minute hand, or some cardboarded space holding a decapitated doll. So, I'm going to leave things the way they are. I'm going to pretend I find myself with the spin of a palindrome: dried up I recount where I scarcely draw myself things that can be so unrecognizable, like a glimpsed piece of wax might be (from what era of my life?), or a connotation with no apparent depth, still like a pardon, in this moment, I have no idea how it can help me.

There are great pieces of life that are only useless.

What I'm Being

Begin, I begin with a trickle: it's that, a trickle I identify with. It could have been some numbers, perhaps, but I confess that, in my case, there is no number.

The big, green stain, the big, yellow-green stain, yes. Yes, that is, in front of my eyes, a constant.

So I have the big stain. The stain I can indeed count on, still I get tangled, yes,

and I get tangled in a void I don't even know how to identify as mine.

Sometimes... like in the Theatre: I could be on a pedestal, but that would only be for a few seconds. Or the way... a way like one from a silent movie?

Well in spite of everything I chew, undoubtedly, a word. A word, in a spectral bathtub, lit up by the white, or in the corner of a memory, very similar to a small, sophisticated box.

Old tremblings, we could say, that have stayed pleated, wrinkled. Senseless, mouldy. Where, here, there's no way out.

Or to slip on a tedious, noisy... Discourse, which... Yet this, in the end, could turn out to be ridiculous. Which is what I say, which is what I'm saying, which is where I submerge myself, until seeing what all this on one day, or another, might get to, or might mean, or it might just be some other thing dilapidatedly out.

Roberto Friol

Mysteries

Another log on the fire
                of history,
                                another truth,

another mystery
           of brightening
                        the face,
of darkening it,
           of making a bundle of reason,
                                    of fear.
On the day
           in history nods
                      your night,
nod
           the words
           to convoke and reunite
           to unite
the one who senses the stream
of reasons
               with the blazing blood
               of having been,
               of becoming
log on the fire
           of the country,
                        of the homeland,
around which
           we sit
                      mysterious.

The Double Face

Yes, they are the same words with another identity,
another fit. And when they come to mind,
what can I do but give myself over to their uproar,
their silence? Home of good mornings,
sullen nights and
how much wanting to be, how much
staying transfigures. Happiness
in shadows, the discourse
of quieting and sleeplessness. This news
is a gift; this waiting,
my double face.

Before a Chinese Pencil

Scent of sandalwood tree this pencil's wood has,
of China, timeless, of tea, of my friends from youth.
Its painted crabs
on the pink skin of conquest
help the sleep coming slowly
upon the soul's snowfall.
Who made it for me not knowing me?
Who with able hands
smoothed and painted the wood,
changed the graphite to obedience,
fortified the corrector of errors?
Who mutters through it,
'The rice joined us from far off,
the reverence to the immortal age,
the tapestry of perfect jades'?
What artisan, heir to the flower,
with this pencil, has entered my life,
my night, the wall of my farewell?

Francisco de Oraá

As if They Kicked You Out of Sleep

One more day now night. One more day
to know I'm stuck now in the bottomless night,
to think, what's become of my life,
or go over what's life done with my life.
I keep wasting streets like a dog
and I don't leave the dark noise of my head,
still I fall,
with all my eyes I fall in the quieted corner of the inn
to contemplate time curdled on my bachelor plate,
dreaming of smoke, patient like insipid pastry,
pondered one by one like taciturn beans,
but making it understood we know how to treat time with dignity.

One more day to jump from sleep
as if they'd kicked you out pushing from its shadow
and doomed to repeat yourself the whole damn day
like you fell from love, choked by disgust
and turning stupider than a hollow,
now no longer able to fathom who thought up this joke;
still in the parks you realize your life is a mistake
happening in someone else's mouth
with a person's shape and a dark heart like a dead man,
crossing a dream in beggar's clothing
(tell the sleeping
they know full well we're tangled up with death
that the dead laugh seeing us stuck halfway in death)
and you still ask yourself how you've got to be: – on the quiet
sort out a joke with life
and make it understood you treat death with dignity.

Dry

I would visit the bum-legged sailor to see that frigate above the door, now useless from the dust and with a topmast like a mind suffering birds: at night a roar of waters moving the dark breezes of another world, and it had become disillusioned with the dawn. That boat made it rain.

On Three Photos of Mella

At home there was a photo of Mella on the wall
like in others the taut faces of saints.
Then I was a boy sprawled in the yard.
Something fascinated me: I felt a gentle strangeness when
     considering
that headstrong profile
leaving for a future beginning in its skin,
an aggressive seriousness,
perhaps sullen, elusive, disrespectful to me
like a tree condensed in its hardness,
its proud tendon about to burst.

Years later a friend dedicated a photo to me where you could see
     Mella head-on
but in his frown of a scolding father I seemed to hear Mella asking
     me darkly:
'What are you doing about the world? What are you doing with
     your life?'
I responded as my strange being allowed –
always strange to everyone else and far from my own desire,
so I wasn't what I wanted to be
and I didn't live like I would've liked to live.
I only know that, deep down, I would've always liked to be lying
     around the yard,
for the yard to spread out to be the whole world.
Would it have been enough to know I could never put on that
     broad-brimmed hat
Mella has on in the third photo I saw in the papers,
the hat of a man panting beneath the sun,
shrinking the sky down to a horseman's head,
a warrior's cool roof?
Perhaps my part was only to be in love with a yard,
to believe in the meantime those images of an upside down yard in
     the sky would relieve the world's disgrace
and the world would start walking toward the yard.

*Now sometimes I'm ashamed at fifty
of so much life I lost.
Yet Mella, still so young...*

January 11, 1980

Pablo Armando Fernández

The Rooster of Pomander Walk

V

It was that instant when I saw my adversary and in his
hands the keys that would open the gates to the cemeteries,
the instant of my absolution.
What would I do without my fear?
I tried to hold his scornful hand, but my eyes
were tired of perishing and returned to sleep.
My adversary was much happier, it's true, he looked down on
living. He sang in a country of bitter snows.
He kept innocence with his life.
Oh, frightful beauty!
leave me hungry now, at your feet to make the noises of an
expiatory animal.
I am in you, time does not include me.

XI

I read the classics
it's 6:12 am I'm at platform 102 at Grand Central
I don't want to know anything of this immortality
nothing makes me cry.
The Port Chester Local arrives late
arrives full of a servile breathing.
The unfriendly conductor
wanders by pulling out
the mite those who enter vast time
bring beneath their tongues.
I don't want to know anything of this immortality.
He's yelling out Mt. Vernon
and the passengers draw back into the vision.

I would write the Testament of the Twelve Apostles.
It's raining and he's yelling Columbus Avenue
with his indecisive slowness
while I read the Syriac Apocalypse of Baruch.
When it starts to snow again we'll be in Pelham
and I'll have finished the Book of the Secrets of Enoch.
Beneath the trees at the New Rochelle station
are your eyes watching me.
The crying that appears in your eyes
is like the apocryphal Book of Ezekiel.
In Larchmont there's a house lit up
there are invisible meadows
and shadows descending and looking looking looking.
Someone's opened a door
in Mamaroneck so no one can leave.
When the war's over
Harrison will once more be a town with its mothers
who knit and its fathers who go
daily to their businesses meantime
they visit the cemetery.
We've gotten to Rye
I've forgotten again I don't know where to go
if to the dock or the door that's opened
behind me.
Nobody waits for me there.

Nihil Obstat

In his cell Juan de Yepes waits.
The prelates of the Order of Carmelites
are now meeting; Juan made a grave mistake:
he brought into the common tongue the divine canticle.
His brothers in habit give up a few minutes
(they are loaded down with work)
to the arduous inspection of some pages.
They dissect the text
extirpating malignant syllables.
So cautious (may God save them)
concerning the spiritual health
of the parishioners, they go to great lengths
to discover evil, to banish it
from the innocent brotherhood of serfs.
They smiled satisfied, while Juan, in his cell
lives the solitude of wounded love.
The magistrates' teeth shine,
polished by cheese, wine, and apples,
while Juan, in his cell,
bread and water he dines without delay.
The prelates of the Order of Carmelites
have done their duty. They return to their carriages,
while Juan, in his cell,
will endure the disease of cureless love.

Salt of Memory

for Mariano Arias

Fortunate the one who at the root
has within hand's reach
the flower.
The sediment of centuries cuts
the tutelary home into the stone.
By those rooms does one enter
the labyrinth
where light scatters its enigmas.
Fortunate the one who in the pyramidal
centre
founds the rising stairs.
In the beginning was writing
the stellar signs of continuity.
There rest the codes of knowledge:
the mountain and the river.
Fortunate the one who finds
his fulfillment in sap
and aspires to the spiraling perfume
of the flower formed by stars.

Fayad Jamís

Sleepless Man's Rounds

III

The neighbour's dog uselessly bites the chimes.
I'm only awake and have no children or fire.
The churches break away marvellously.
The trembling lark grows light, with its thread colours pink the
    blackest windows.
In another time I would've whistled and the dogs would've come
and a dream would grow in the distant tongues of my feet.
Yet today I wonder, Who am I? What's my name?
Where is my river of blue stones, my tender part
marked off by doves and fire and hope?
Oh, I wander throatless, bodiless,
among these tunnels of panting and howls, absence and misfortune.

V

Oh the doors!
Among the lamps and murmuring dust
the vegetal wall, the paravans of warm mahogany, the invisible
hinges of oblivion ceaselessly creaking.
Do you know? I can knock where it's solid like on the forehead of a
    sleeping man;
the echo caresses me. In the corners of the light
a girl who watches and disappears erases my boredom.
I have my soul tied up like a beast,
burning, next to my feet, my soul of tender rancor
wounded at times by madness!
Do you know? I cross the doors in the evening
like a loving word.

For This Freedom

For this freedom of song beneath the rain
we'll need to give it all
For this freedom of being closely tied
to the sweet, steady insides of the people
we'll need to give it all
For this freedom of sunflower open in the dawn of factories
 switched on and schools lit
and of earth creaking and child awakening
we'll need to give it all
There is no alternative but freedom
There is no other way but freedom
There is no other homeland but freedom
There will be no more poem if not for the violent music of
 freedom
For this freedom which is the fear
of those who always violated it
in the name of magnificent miseries
For this freedom which is the night of the oppressors
and the definitive dawn of all the people now invincible
For this freedom revealing the sunken pupils
     the bare feet
     the leaky roofs
     and the eyes of children who
     wandered in the dust
For this freedom which is the empire of youth
For this freedom
beautiful like life
we'll need to give it all
if necessary
even shadow
and it will never be enough

Better to Get Up

If you can't sleep get up and sail.
If you still don't know how to die keep learning to love.
The early morning doesn't close your world, outside there are stars,
hospitals, huge machines unsleeping.
Outside there is your soup, the warehouse that nourishes your senses,
your city's wind. Get up and turn on
the turbines of your soul, don't get tired of walking
everywhere, take note of the final filth
remaining in your land, since everything transforms
and you no longer have eyes for abolished horror.
Get up and multiply the windows, spit on the faces of
the incredulous: for them every greenness is nothing more than rust.
Shoot off your victor's tongue, don't only wait for the peaceful table
while in other places in the world murderers shriek.

If you can't dream batter the dusty trunks.
If you still don't know how to live don't teach how to live in vain.
Crush reality, wear out your shoes auscultating the streets,
don't give any hand-outs. Get up and help the world to awaken.

Roberto Fernández Retamar

The Ugly Ones

to Alejo Carpentier

The immortal hand or eye
That made the starry sky, this bay,
This restaurant, this table,
(And even Blake's tiger)
Also made her, and it made her ugly.
Something in her eyes, or nose,
Her mouth just slightly too small,
Or a forehead cut short before its time
By her hair of a perplexing colour;
Something insurmountable forever
Fighting off powder and lipstick,
Makes it so tonight, next to the bay,
At El Templete Restaurant,
Tonight with soft sea breezes
And red wine and friendship,
She is alone at a table,
Peering perhaps into her bowl of soup
At the unsteady image of her face,
Her ugly face forcing
the order of the entire universe to falter,
Until an ugly man appears
And sits at her table.

You Were Right, Tallet: We Are Men of Transition

Between the whites whose blood you can see circulating, when they are almost polar, past their eyes, beneath their straw-coloured hair,
And the nocturnal blacks, sometimes blue, chosen and purified by horrible tests, so only the best survived and they are the lone truly superior race on the planet;
Between those who were startled by the bomb that first made the lamps blink and later finished off in a young man hanging from a corner pole,
And those who learn to live with the song *marching we go towards an ideal*, and spell out Camilo (perhaps younger than us) like we do Ignacio Agramonte (as old now as the Egyptians when we went to the first classrooms);
Between those who had to wait, their hands sweating, for a job, for any job,
And those who can choose and turn down jobs without swallowing their pride, or lying or falling silent, and there are jobs no one wants to do now for money, and volunteers have to go (we have to go) so that the country continues living;
Between the spattered weaknesses, Saint Peter's denials, almost every day on almost every street,
And the heroism of those who've scattered their names throughout schools, farms, defence committees, factories, etc.;
Between a class we didn't belong to, because we couldn't go to their schools and didn't believe in their gods,
And weren't in charge in their offices or didn't live in their homes or dance in their halls or swim at their beaches or make love together or say hello to each other,
And another class where we asked for a place, but we don't have all their same Memories and we don't have all their same humiliations,
And it points with its hardened, swollen hands, forever deformed,
To our hands polished by paper or moved around by numbers;
Between the tormented discovery of pleasure,
The electric glory of bodies and shame, the fear of not doing it well,

of not going to do it well,
And the height of beauty and grace, the beautiful possession of a woman by a man, of a girl by a boy,
Chosen for each other like fruit, like truths in light;
Between the sleeplessness chewed by the clock on the wall,
The hand that cannot sign the grade sheet or bring the damn spoonful of soup to the mouth,
The fear of fear, the tears of deaf, powerless fear,
And the joy of one welcoming into the body the day's hard-working fatigue and the night's just rest,
Of one lifting tools and weapons, and too a beloved body trembling from illusion, without giving it a thought,
Between believing tons of things, about the earth, heaven, and hell,
And believing absolutely nothing, not even that the doubter truly exists;
Between the certainty that everything is one great trap, a colossal joke, and what the hell are we doing here, and what is here,
And the hope that things can be different, ought to be different, will be different;
Between what we don't want to be anymore, and would've preferred not to be,
And what we'd like to be still,
And what we want, what we hope to be one day, if we have time and heart and insides;
Between some neighbourhood hotshot, Roenervio for example, who could always do more than you, god dammit,
And José Martí, who exalted and shamed, shining like a star;
Between the past where, obviously, we hadn't been, and so it was past,
And the future where we weren't going to be either, and so it was future,
Even though we were the past and the future, since if not for us they wouldn't exist.
And, naturally, we don't want (and we know we won't get) pity or pardon or sympathy,
Perhaps not even understanding, from the better men to come later, who should come later, history's not for that,
But for us to live it wholly, without openings, if possible

(Still with love, since it's likely to be the one true thing).
And the dead will be dead, with their clothes, their books, their
 conversations, their dreams, their pains, their sighs, their
 glories, their trivialities.
And since we too have been history, and we too have built
 happiness, beauty, and truth, and we've been present in the light,
 as today we form part of the present.
And since, after all, comrades, who knows
If only the dead aren't men of transition.

Heberto Padilla

Cuban Poets No Longer Dream

Cuban poets no longer dream
                            (not even at night).

They're closing the door to write alone
when the wood suddenly creaks;
the wind shoves them down the drain;
some hands grab them by the shoulders,
turn them over,
        put them face to face with other faces

(sunken in swamps burning in napalm)
and the world above their mouths flows
and the eye is forced to see, to see, to see.

The Man on the Edge

He's not the man jumping the barrier
already feeling seized by his time, or the fugitive
hidden in the coach panting
or fleeing among terrorists, or the poor
man with a cancelled passport
who's always lying in wait for a border.
He lives closer to heroism
(in that dark part):
still he doesn't go mad, get startled.
He doesn't want to be a hero,
not even the romantic you could
weave a legend around;
still he's condemned to this life and, what terrifies him most,
fatally to his era.
He's a decapitated man in the dead of night, drifting from one room to the next,
like an enormous wind barely surviving the outside wind.
Each morning he begins again
(like Italian actors).
He suddenly stands as if someone snatched his character.
No mirror
        would dare copy
this fallen lip, this knowledge gone broke.

Offside

to Yiannis Ritsos, in a Greek prison

The poet, release him!
There's nothing left for him to do here.
He's not in the game.
Doesn't get carried away.
Doesn't make his message clear.
Doesn't even make out miracles.
Spends the entire day musing.
Always finds something to object to.

That fellow, release him!
Get rid of the spoilsport,
summer's
ill-tempered man,
with dark glasses
beneath the rising sun.
He was
always seduced by wanderings
and beautiful catastrophes
of time without History.
He's
    even
        outdated.
Only likes good old Armstrong.
Hums, at most,
a song by Pete Seeger.
Sings,
under his breath
                Guantanamera.

Still there's
nobody who can make him open his mouth,
still there's

nobody who can make him smile
each time the show begins
and the clowns
leap through the scene;
when the cockatoos
mix up love and terror
and the stage creaks
and the brass and drums
thunder
and everybody leaps,
leans,
steps back,
smiles,
opens their mouths
    'Why yes,
    yes, of course,
    yes indeed...'
And they all dance well,
they dance nice,
just the way the dance asks them to.
That fellow, release him!
There's nothing left for him to do here.

César López

The tablecloths and sheets hung out moved with the wind, afterward
    the hand,
the hand that could make things more varied, devoted itself to writing
a letter. There's always a distant relative who needs writing to.
Yet the letter carefully deposited in the mailbox, a little
dirty from the grazing, revealed the hands' first activity.
Those were not the poet's hands. But it was a letter
where acts, maternal worries were told.
The city was always full of mothers. Their steps keeping an eye out
and the constant exercise of determining the children's trailed tasks.
That was not the poet's letter. And the poet hadn't been invited.
Actually there was no party the poet
should have been invited to. Still it so happens
that the poet appeared precisely after the movement
of tablecloths and sheets hung out, when night fell
and the covered patio remained deserted and only with the stains
and the gentle scent of recently laundered clothes.
The poet was the son of a widow who was quite comfortably off.
They never wondered what would be
the poet's function in the city. He wasn't
surrounded enough by the things he asked for either, namely:
a pond inhabited with lotuses and transparent fish, various
daffodils recently cut, a pink seashell and more belatedly
a set of Tarot cards; nobody understood
why he would ask for onions, ropes, sharks, a compass rose
or from the winds, vampires, three albino women, and an invisible
    suitcase.
Anyway, since the poet needed too many things, the people
decided to not take him seriously. And they stopped worrying.
They decided to ignore him (it's very difficult to be so precise
when people are pretending). And sometimes they'd watch him walk
    down Marina
Street, for example, laden with books or dreams, and nobody
commented on his work and his sweat or anything because the poet

was also very skinny. Perhaps nobody knew he was the poet.
Still the mother was completely terrified and decided
to consult someone who would know, and after some doubts went to
 see a laundry woman (clean clothes were always a revealing sign for
 the poet)
who had much light to shed on these cases. The mother read to her
something of what the son had denominated poems, and the good
 laundry woman
determined that the poet had a backward spirit following him.
Cologne prepared especially for him, baths with leaves,
herbs and other accessories, doves, coins, and the poet
never understood very well such a move, and mostly
white clothes, so many clean clothes.
The poet at that time was obsessed with equinoxes,
which were undoubtedly more mysterious than vulgar solstices,
and he followed them with his imagination flying high
until they appeared in all his poems. He believed in magic
and didn't know more of love than some sighs of exacerbated lyricism.
He did know the sea, but never learned to swim.
The poet was twenty years old. When he was alone
and friendless, nobody greeted him, and so nobody
knew he was a poet… With the exception of his mother and the
 laundry woman.
So he walked around looking at mountains, a cloud
or a listless girl who unsettled him (in these cases
he masturbated later like a condemned man).
One night, it was early morning when an infinity of things
might occur, buried in a stormy reading of William Blake,
almost naked, between the blankets and sheets moving with the wind,
the poet yelled out excitedly. *So what? Excited… Excited.*
Alone he yelled out to the world, to the city. He was the poet.
And so he paid no attention to the opening door. To the blue
uniforms, to the blows and to the rapid bursts of machine guns
that crossed his chest and waist…
So died the poet, the neighbours next door, suspicious (those were the
 times)
had given the notice to the police. The thugs
destroyed everything they found in the house. The mother and the

      laundry woman
were the only ones left. They both cried. (This is what the letter says.)
The tablecloths still, the sheets, now hanging in shreds.
The fresh stains of his blood. The wind.
There were always clean clothes in his destiny; and some things the city
    ignores.

Minute, tiny park, somber and quiet,
people always pass by there in a hurry,
almost no lingering, no noticing its discrete charm;
and still it was like a veiled place
that cared and helped the city. Morning,
noon, evening, *la noche
se puso íntima como una pequeña plaza*. So,
meager, scarce benches, earth;
with vegetation hiding its designs
and some old beggar or perhaps a
hasty conversation and something hushed.
Surrounded by life's constant signs,
but left to the edge; crossroads,
hidden Elegguá, deciphered
square of destiny, orienter
of ways more closed than open.
No chronicle or profile to distinguish it.

On one side is the power of governments
and the collectors of taxes or rather their memory.
There's the bare, pretentious, proud temple.
Stores elegant, exotic, foreign,
charming, yet all empty,
like beholden cantons in vigil.
A bar with its tall, wobbly stools,
the mirror and resounding noise of constant music.

And at a gentle decline, lightly prolonged,
the house of death and the dead
in a perpetual traffic of boxes and coffins,
and the blue bus stations echoing
transitory exits. Escape from the annoyance.
How the past dreams! How imprecise
the unwritten chronicle! The strange inventions.

All this area summons up the exit to the city,
by different routes, by ways
of dust and snags – *verte y no verte* – ,

with omens, trembles, and anxieties
por caminos sin agua va tu agonía.

It has to do with such a tiny centre,
not a fundamental nucleus of the city,
yet it's indispensible to jot down
its memory at least. It is and no longer is.
To be or not to be. Tell me the story.
*To have and have not. Anda, camina,
camina, Juan Pescao. Camina pa'lante...*
Nobody returns to the past. To the fizzy
soft drinks from the corner soda fountain,
to the fake bubbles of the times.
Tea for two and two for tea.
Oh, if this were possible, how much weariness
and what of terrible, frustrating things
would be discovered by the perpetual inhabitants
of the city destroyed, broken, atrocious confabulary!
In the old days, when carriages or cars
scarcely stopped their march down that bustling street
of Enramadas and faces and waists
sweetly swaying, nobody
or rather almost nobody, remembered its name.

– Small plaza, minute park –

Why should they do it now, city,
if these days heat, suffocating history,
count for so very few.

Rafael Alcides Pérez

The Grateful One

to Naty Revuelta

My whole life's been a disaster
I don't regret.
No childhood made me a man
and love upholds me.

Prison, hunger, everything,
everything's been just fine:
the backstabs in the night
and the unknown father.

And so from what I didn't have
was born this, what I am:
really not much, it's true,
yet giant, grateful like a dog.

1963

A Man and a Woman

A man and a woman walk down the street. And
they laugh. Make plans.
It went well at the hotel where they made love
and they laugh, make a date for tomorrow. Life is grand.
Tomorrow he'll be laid out at the funeral home an hour
before the date (the scaffolding
on the top floor loosened at ten fifty-five)
and three years later she's checked into the hospital,
for only a few days, nothing
serious
(this is how she'll say it on the phone the afternoon before
to her friends: who already know it's cancer).
But now they've just made love,
they have a date for tomorrow, and they laugh, hold
hands. It's been an amazing afternoon.
They wouldn't trade places with anyone.

Nobody

To immortalize him
they raised a statue.
Later, time passed,
the wars, the exoduses
arrived. Occupied
and plundered ceaselessly,
the city knew fire
one century after another,
and the ashes from its flames
floated over the ruins
leaving a snowy colour
throughout the millennium.
On a whim,
for reasons of State
or to take it away as a trophy
upon a mule's back, perhaps
an invader
stripped the statue
of the powerful plaque
that prolonged the distinguishing features
of that immortal.
Yet the statue held out.
Frightened, it is there still,
a traveller, ever standing,
watching eternity pass,
all of eternity
in a little park famous
and now immemorially:
'Nobody's little park.'

Antón Arrufat

Metals

What do you think of the word metal?
Do you like it?
If I say,
the metal of your voice,
do you like it?
Metal sounds,
shimmers, endures.
Gleams in the dirt
of excavations.
'It's a metal,' says
the Egyptologist's helper.
A metal in Etruria,
in Uxmal,
in the remote
city of Ur.
A metal,
the metal of your voice.

At the Son's Door

'Come in. Here too are the gods.'
So my mother, the cook, is a goddess?
Hey, old lady, guess what, you're the goddess of the stove.
Your scent is the scent of the goddesses of Homer.
Move destiny with your spoon,
receive as offerings garlic
and the pot's wet whistles.
The frying pan is a round, black flower.
Look at the knives hanging like altar candles,
but careful they don't cut your finger
or sink into your sacred chest.
(The frying pan is a round, black flower.)
Sorry your greasy face arrives late
to summer, rain, grown children.
A goddess doesn't abandon her temple.
On and on at the altar mother.
For you myths have not been made.

Apology in Detail

Out of fear
the man built a house
set sail
vanquished the tyrant
who walked along insolently
out of fear
of being poisoned in his bedroom
Out of fear
we dress a certain way
inherit the gestures
the voice of the dead
we frequent dogma
on our knees
we say 'see you soon'
'see you later'
to entangle death
in the word
we invent eternity
to find ourselves
after so many farewells
Out of fear
we don't accept our bodies
our feelings
the love of a sister
freedom
trains leaving
Out of fear
someone leaves in search
of the snitch
and finishes him in the shadows
Out of fear
we make our image
out of others
heroes or traitors
Out of fear

someone seeks
his death
favours it
flatters it
wants a timid peace
Out of fear
we love one another furiously
provoke the ire
of the enemy
we were angry
arbitrary and sad
Out of fear
we raise a city
kill the tiger
in the deep jungle
the dream tiger
the nightmare tiger
the man dressed
as a beast
the old beasts
from the circus
Out of fear
we learned
to live
on the tightrope
fear
later
changed it to art
Out of fear

Manuel Díaz Martínez

Leave

Leave the moon
and dogs in the yard;
leave the chrysanthemums
in the lone glass pitcher;
leave the suede mask
beneath my bed;
leave my weapons a handspan from me
and the wind in the roads;
leave me upon this thick notebook
where I write
the words you forget.

The House

The workers came to demolish the house.
    They began
by removing the doors and dismantling the windows.
    Later
they raised the floors and placed the tiles in rows
    on the yard's yellow grass.

The workers knew how to do things; they moved
    from side to side, no smiling or talking,
    insatiably carrying, hitting,
    dragging, forcing, demolishing.

Finally, they brought down the roof and walls.

Where we had found sleep and a family air
    blew became a landscape of upturned earth,
    splintered sticks, lime, and sun.

The workers gathered up their tools,
    happy with their labour, and left the
    house carefully closing windows and
    doors.

Immortals

We are truly strong:
harder than river rock,
than the steel from a coastal cannon,
than the jiquí
              the ácana
                            and the black júcaro trees.

There's no engine
– turbo reactor or diesel –
more potent than us,
or lacquer or synthetic fibre
more tenacious than us.
We know
        love
        hate
and especially
passion and hope:
how to doubt that of the things on Earth
we are
the strongest?
We've seen pass by our side
packs of colossal beasts
never to reappear,
we still see the light from stars now ghosts,
entire continents sank beneath our feet
to not return from the bottom
of the ocean,
above our livid heads
pass by
species of birds and airplanes
that do not pass by again.
                        Yet we,
poor creatures with no claws or shells
or scales or quills or wings,
with eyes inferior to an owl's eyes

and legs inferior to a moose's legs
and hands inferior to a monkey's tiny hands
and an ear inferior to the mockingbird's
and a sense of smell inferior to a dogfish's
and muscles much poorer, much weaker
than the boa's elastic muscles...
     Yet we,
the most fragile,
the least protected,
               asthmatic
               arthritic
               diabetic
               near-sighted,
we've survived all the catastrophes,
all the iniquities,
               our very selves.

José Kozer

My Father, Who Is Still Alive

My father, who is still alive,
I don't see him, and I know he's grown smaller,
has a family of charred brothers in Poland,
never saw them, found out about his mother's death by telegram,
didn't inherit even a button from his father,
how should I know if he inherited his character.
My father, who was a tailor and a Communist,
my father who didn't speak and sat on the terrace
to not believe in God,
to want nothing more to do with men,
brooding against Hitler, brooding against Stalin,
my father who once a year threw back a glass of whisky,
my father sitting by a neighbour's apple tree eating the fruit
the day the reds entered his town,
and they made my grandfather dance like a bear on a Saturday,
and they made him light a cigarette and smoke it on a Saturday,
and my father left the village forever,
left forever grumbling about the October Revolution,
forever insisting Trotsky was a fool and Beria a criminal,
denouncing books he sat down so small on the terrace,
and told me men's dreams are nothing more than a false literature,
history books lie because paper withstands it all.
My father who was a tailor and a Communist.

On the Nation

In Cuba a crimson rain fell.

I smell of remains, the red rain soaks the hindquarters of a mare grazing among the nettles and a pleasure's burrs.

The water doesn't get me wet, I don't understand it, the red water.

What tree is that at the corner of the house? Why do they give a warning cry that by virtue of its shape it's a fir or a birch, that you can see a forest of trembling aspens climbing the mountain?

The mountain? This neighbourhood, isn't it the one they call La Víbora, isn't Santo Suárez there?

Four movie theatres, two avenues crossed, a large number of patriots, every house a yard every yard two flowerpots of rosy periwinkle always on either side of the third step to the entrance, is it around here?

I smell of blindness, a stale scent, I can sense that soon I'll smell of snuff, the ammonia of synagogues, scent of a dying man, will I return?

Did it clear up? It doesn't clear up. New once more for me are these atmospheric phenomena, you could say my own life a thermic inversion, on the bias the drizzle smells suddenly of tobacco, the flan in the kitchen is curdled and smells of caramel put to cool on the cedar board on the table.

And they swing her and swing her, it creaks, green poles, green wood recently painted the two seats of the swing on the terrace, which of them? Three there were three: Perla, Ana, or Esther?

Auntie, why Esther with an h? Funny, how funny the explanations.

Look at me, I draw two initials: look at me, blotting paper: I am handwriting.

And from the red rain nothing grows in Cuba the crimson soil has dried out.

I'm going to start listening, however long it takes I'm going to start listening. They say, I know from the diction, from the Havana accent they say chameleon, sticky nightshade they say, they said (at the top of their lungs) I'm coming, they knocked on the door.

The knocker's tall, wide door, I knocked with my knuckles, it's raining (when will I get wet?) wood dust fell, a good piece of masonry, urine and urine, I look up, the four of us peep out in our thick, verdigris terrycloth robes (it thundered) the spaces opened, we rubbed our eyes and saw a railing in its first apparition, the geometrical edgings of a tablecloth, all at once the light through the mullion's window, and through the light the bougainvillea climbing.

Miguel Barnet

Revolution

for Roberto Fernández Retamar

When the revolution arrived
the crowd entered my home
It seemed to rifle through the drawers, the closet,
change the sewing basket

That old silence ceased
and my grandmother stopped weaving memories,
she stopped speaking,
she stopped singing

Hopeful I saw, had to see,
how the light entered that room
when my mother opened the windows
for the very first time

Orishas

The orishas dance with wire masks
and eat on grass mats

The orishas speak through the oracle
while the dogs howl from the
four cardinal points

The orishas enter the monte-ewe
anchored to their beautiful trophies
and their copper lamps

The orishas feel an awful blow to the stomach
and demand their ration of food
feel a strange boiling in their blood
and demand their ration of justice

The orishas can walk on just one foot
hear with just one ear
and speak their ancient words
lipless
mouthless

The orishas enter the monte-finda
with their eyes
like two squashes set afire
and there's no possible dream
or morning with light
to make a new arch burst
on the roundness of the earth

The orishas carry out their unchanging destiny – opal or mist –
and return victorious
to their dances of love
whistling their throaty whistles

Man of this era
don't be fooled
Those who tether the horizon to their waists
and spin barbarous solitary
on their own heads
aren't men
but orishas

Miami

Miami is a question of visiting.
Miami, Gustavo Pérez Firmat was right,
'is a rocket loaded with future,
it's a lot of commotion and little motion.'
And not everything's in black and white, there's grey tint
– it's quite abundant actually –
light pink and even bright red.
In Miami nothing Cuban is alien, except Cuba.
Miami, it's worthwhile mentioning, is a linguistic paradise.
It's Noah's Ark, with ducks and crocodiles.
But there's culture in Miami.
There's the Calvin Klein House of Culture,
the Gucci House of Culture,
and the McDonald's House of Culture.
Everything in Miami is blue and sound machine
and they call you 'para atrás' and they tell you 'bye'
and they decorate you with gold chains with a huge
Santa Barbara and a ruby the size of the diamond in the Capitolio.
But Miami has its Coconut Grove, its Ocean Drive,
and its esquina de Tejas.
Miami is so pretty at night!
When I look in the eyes of the Cubans in Miami,
I see my Uncle Javier, my cousin Margarita,
all my relatives happy to be living in Miami, Fla.
But me, just passing through, I'm sad.
Could it be I don't like paradise?
Could it be I prefer hell?
Miami confuses me.
Por ejemplo, when I go to Calle Ocho,
so pretty, so many restaurants,
I lose my appetite.
Could it be there are too many dishes, too many options?
Or could it be my grandmother shows up at La Carreta
like the ghost of Hamlet's father,
with three twists of a costume jewellery necklace

and imprudent bags under her eyes.
Miami confuses me.
Miami's happiness confuses me.
Could I be losing my taste for happiness?
What to do with so much confusion?
The radio in Miami has a permanent open mic
and it's a treatise on scatological linguistics: the word mierda,
the word carajo, the word... they say it all point-blank.
In Miami just look how words are heavy.
In Miami just look how confusion is heavy.
Just look how the heart is heavy.
In spite of it all.

My room is dark
and the air conditioning moans
in earnest.

I get up too early
because my dog relentlessly barks,
I turn on the TV to get
a bit of light and buzz
to turn off my dog's barking
and the air conditioning's noise.

But my dog keeps at it and I go to the front
door to confirm the void, the nothingness.

Then I pet his back,
I quiet him so I can sleep.

Why hadn't I thought before that he was only
barking at me!

Luis Rogelio Nogueras

P4R

> *From the hands of peasants quickly appears furniture in the purest Russian style. At other times there are modernist chess games, the pieces are no longer the classic towers, queen, king [...] but on one side the 'whites' (the bourgeois man, the bourgeois woman, the czarist official, the church tower) and on the other the reds (the worker, the peasant woman, the red soldier, the anvil, etc.)*
> Julio A. Mella, *Portraits of the Soviet Union*

No special sign marks the spot today
– undoubtedly historical in the voluminous history of
    coincidences –
where, practically strangers,
concentrating beyond future, vocation,
war, the unsteady order of the universe,
the Bolshevik and the Dadaist,
at Zurich's old Café Terrassein 1916,
moved horses, bishops, towers, kings.
In the strict layout of the anecdote
we only know Lenin lived on The Spiegelgasse
at number 2,
and at number 1, in the Cabaret Voltaire,
the Dadaists met to talk about the dynamism of Freedom,
of drawers full of brains, of the sacred cow's tail,
of the bucket and the mother, of the wooden horse,
of eroticism, of instinct.
Other facts – how they dressed, who won the match – are lost,
whisked away by more decisive events,
crushed by time's unquestionable weight.
Now we can only imagine the words exchanged,
after checkmate,
what each thought while moving the black and white pieces

according to a strategy tactically agreed upon,
so much that coincidence, or whatever it was, moved them,
the Bolshevik and the Dadaist, on the enormous
board of possibilities, facing them off.
Later, they probably limited themselves to smiling,
analyzed the match
('better Pawn Four Queen and then Bishop Four Bishop for
    Pawn Three King')
shook hands, and then perhaps drank a few beers;
not knowing a thing about the other,
except they were exiles,
since Zurich was at that time the refuge for all political
    immigrants,
international smugglers, ex-ministers,
deserters,
out of work violinists,
painters,
naturalists,
somber Spanish,
squalid pacifists.
Each of us is free to imagine history in our own way
because they, who could have told it
didn't know or didn't want to; they wanted to make it,
walking blindly, busy building or saying
things so that afterwards
the biographers
could mix everything up.
I prefer to think of them saying things perhaps they never said,
swearing, laughing, drinking beer
the Bolshevik and the Dadaist,
each waiting his turn,
Lenin,
to cross the border by train in the night
and with that journey to change History
with a single blow,
and Tzara,
to arrive in Paris,
shake hands with Breton and begin his

scream scream scream scream scream scream scream
scream scream scream scream scream scream scream
scream scream scream scream scream scream scream
scream scream scream scream scream scream scream
both,
waiting in between a castling and a beer,
for the moment to kick
out once and for all from the kingdom
of men,
the towers,
the bishops,
the queens,
the kings.

Joe Bell/The Inspector's Last Case

Due to a lack of proof, no alternative remains but to accept as legitimate the thesis that has now been daringly upheld by the English critic Thomas Hogarth for over the past thirty years: 'Murder' was written by Conan Doyle's old Grammar teacher Joe Bell, in whose sharp face, extravagant tastes, and curious ability to notice certain details Sherlock Holmes is, in part, inspired.

Very little is known of this Bell. Hogarth himself can only offer us scarce concrete facts about the enigmatic model for the immortal Holmes. The trump card raised by the English critic to defend his thesis is a brief note, appearing on the corresponding page on Tuesday, February 11, 1888 in the ledger of the now defunct London newspaper *Express*, where the following was recorded:

> '17 guineas were paid B/O Mr. Joe Bell, author of the poem 'Murder,' which appeared in the 8-2 edition signed by William Bliot, pseud[onym]'

Hogarth confirms that the editor of *Express*, Sir Gilbert Cuff, was a close friend of Doyle's and that, most likely, it was the latter who sent off the small poem by his old teacher.

The translation (in free verse) of 'Murder' has been done by Samuel Espada, who's preferred to entitle it: 'The Inspector's Last Case':

The scene of the crime
is still not the scene of the crime:
it's only a dimly lit room
where two naked shadows kiss.

The killer
is still not the killer:
he's only a weary man
who's going home a day before expected,
after a long journey.

The victim
is still not the victim:
she's only a woman burning
in other arms.

The special witness
is still not the special witness:
he's only a bold inspector
enjoying his neighbour's wife
in his neighbour's bed.

The crime weapon
is still not the crime weapon:
>it's only a bronze lamp switched off,
>calm, innocent
>on the mahogany table.

Nancy Morejón

Mutisms IV

A circle. A duende. A mirror.
Immediately me.
From that tortuous seat
in search of me you come.
                What do you seek
                below my black line
                hiding
                though it wants to hold?
There is no hope. There is no pain.
I am without me. And I fly against you,
wind,
dragging perhaps the inutterable
toward your noise.

Carpet

for Lourdes Casal

The idea of a poem
comes in through the window,
perhaps perfumed, with no notice.
Did I maybe manage to fool
so much lost longing...?
It's as if a carpet,
as if someone placed
a carpet at my feet
and now steady I could take
sharp flight, with the benevolence
of that reader whose dream nested
the reading of Boti...
I can't...
Oh steady dream,
oh clear sails toward my red body...
And the idea of the poem
is no longer,
is no longer.

The Golden Chair

to the memory of Loló Soldevilla

I'm a faceless little woman
sitting on the tip of a rock,
toward the bottom of a landscape
where a river and two seas are found.
I can't stop contemplating them:
a river for two seas, two seas for a river;
until the gannet's cry,
beyond the clouds, awakens them.
I can't speak, I have no hands.
An age-old whip slowly cut them off.
And I scarcely recognize the newly learned words.
I scarcely have a tongue for good morning
and good night.
Everything is immensity around me.
Everything is immense like my hurricane hair
and my grandparents' beastliness:

My grandmother Brígida, drowned in the ink of notaries,
yet invincible, murmuring, and small;
tattooed in the memory of quails,
there in Ciego de Ávila;
fixed in the furies of turbines
where Felipe Morejón Noyola dwelled;
fixed in the memory of Aida Santana, with her honey hatchet;
fixed in my own heart.
My grandmother Ángela, thrashed and singing
decimated by twenty-four births,
thrown to the tenement houses with her sad song,
thrown to the dogs,
thrown to early undeserved death,
like all early deaths,
yet singing a nameless song
in an armless rocking chair, with María Teresa,
'con sus trovas fascinantes que me las quiero aprender.'

Deaths of my grandmothers
I never met.
Deaths of my predatory grandfathers
I never met either.

The willows' leafage calms my worry.
The birds are chirping.
Sitting before this foam,
the memories of La Place Academy splash:
The best student in fourth grade
has the role of a mischievous little black chick
whose brothers and sisters were all little yellow chicks
but the little black chick was the disobedient one,
the sinner, perhaps the true guilty one.
That same student –
barred from studying at the Sorbonne
thanks to some disapproving opinions, wisely hidden,
and above all thanks to the trap set by so many bastards,
interested in proving how unseemly
a little black chick daring to set foot in Paris –
it could never stop being,
never stopped being that little black chick.
I am a faceless little woman.
   The July wind came.
They'd destined me to an old broom and a frying pan,
the last place in line,
a muzzle and the most unaware submission.
They came down hard on me.
They beat me down too.
Blessed the old broom and frying pan,
the last place in line,
a muzzle and apparent submission.
I am a faceless little woman
sitting on the tip of a rock
and the güijes howl in the night
overcome by the July wind
I am who I am on a golden chair.

Raúl Rivero

Pardon This Slight Distraction

I know at this stage of the game
during this period of civilization precisely
poetry shouldn't speak of me
but with me of what is happening.

Still at this stage of the game too
when we must stop looking back
and stare straight ahead
youth and childhood begin to ache
like when someone we love so
starts on a long journey or has just died.

A man is always a bit of his past,
his first moments, his first blow to the face.

Pardon this slight distraction:
I have a friend in bad shape and another set to leave.

Death Suite

I've just been informed I've died.
It's been announced between the lines in the official press.

I wasn't expecting to die this beautiful summer
at the end of the century
but my country's papers never lie
and so this heartbeat is false
the pulsations, the air I breath.

The memories I have are, must be,
my last ravings since the State
doesn't get it wrong so flagrantly.

I've died.
Even I, thirsty and sad,
am beginning to understand it.

I, still loving and astounded and scared,
am learning to die by decree.
Slow, obedient, discreetly, with not one single sign of rage,
I start to look like a cadaver.
To rigorously comply with the order
and not disturb the delight of my executioners
in the spirit of contingency I extinguish
my enduring vital signs
since he who's followed like a sheep
the bell's one rhythm
and the shepherd's voice
must be prepared to die
with only the knife's glare.

II

Mamá already knows
and comes right away to cut my nails

lay a perfumed handkerchief on me
convince Humberto to cut my hair
too long, too white
too calm.

III

Faith is so blind
and so deaf
credibility is so absolute
that the people who see me don't greet me
those who listen to me don't turn their heads
since they've already heard the news
and to those who visit my family
I offer coffee
but they don't thank me
not even a polite phrase, not praise for its bitterness
since this kind of faith
is, what's more, quite tasteless.

As my funeral was made public
along with my sins, my atrocities, my fierce alliances
with the enemy
many people have come to my house to see my plunders
and take with them, if there were, virtue or love.

I've seen them come to offer their condolences
eyeing the furniture and telephone
longing for my coat, the warmth of my bed
sentimental beggars
helping the State nail the lid of my coffin.

I've seen Cristina cry
love shiver
and Mariakarla happy
sure this is another one of my tricks.

I'm a witness to the burial they're giving me.
I was watchful at the wake
and took note of every gesture, every comment.
I've seen everything clearly from my death.

I'm waiting for them.

Lina de Feria

for Ana María Simo

if those who don't want to understand me will so allow
I am like a forest ranger's house
where the hatchet is guilt and the trees fall
and the dust is a light where death writes.
we're at the back of what we sensed
against you that glance will linger established by you
and always thought shameful since it's not lone or complete
it comes from the miserable suburbs of intuition
it's poor and intense like any poor, intense suburban dweller
against you that glance will linger since I remember it like a last god
and I'll remember it beyond the bad poems and this life that won't
    settle down.
after that I began to believe in reality
(a santero would say: after that I had the light brother the light)
the beautiful things took me over
surrounded by flimsy refuges and even by unreal tendernesses
I sought the affirmation of lips until brutality.
all the body's panic startled love
now I know to what point you can be the betrayal of yourself
                              and no one noticing
not the one friend trying to help or the other who doesn't care at all
so I'd like to get away from clumsy handlings
and for example feel that we're more us.
(if those who don't want to understand me will so allow)
make feeling stir suddenly like a catastrophe
give me a manslaughter embrace
run with me toward the unidicting sea.

From María García Granados to José Martí

the stove
a poor sanctuary of coal
cornered in a brief death.
at your back my slippery eyes
conquered by the forehead I loved most
when I held another life corporeal
        and yet equally lonely.

at this great moment
when I watch you seek choose
in the poem's innumerable voices
where to leave my recitable history
for the courtyards of famous civic acts
in the so very private schools of the Republic
and might they always say of me:
        she had the most rupestrian face of the century
and couldn't hide her confusion
when your intelligence had a rein day
                against the wind.

listen to me José Martí
so you avoid once and for all that poem
I am not the ice cadaver
or the cadaver of a love you felt
like the son of flattery
        but instead a hidden ember
burning like your solitude's fire
ember falling ember until the last instant
when I condensed all the river water
as I went inevitably toward the depths.

The Mudslide and the Burial

II

in the morbid dream
that copperwood trunk crosswise in the water
                      distorts the images:

the naked lady
running through the classic ruinous mazes
and the great peacock
now airless looking at
his tail faded with hurricanes and eyes
and the rounds of so many of the same bicycles
like a chopstick before the Stone Judge
and nothing flies nothing
(within the dream I mean)
not even the image of the image
of that horseshoe thrown with credulity
backs to the fountain
on the dolmens and pamphlets
like a kabbalah in the wind
making more powerful the magic of a kind of stupid gesture
yet perhaps destiny's one spindle.

Raúl Hernández Novás

She watched the tall flamboyant trees catch fire.
She named the war fires.
She walks within an eye open like the day.
Breathes and glides her hands over a fabric dark like the night.
In the night she's sewing a flag, she's always sewing it
though the dead have spread their roots to the heart of the earth,
since it's always hope that opens with her eyes.
She is simple, lengthens herself in doves since the evening is mild
when it falls on her shoulders: She grows facing the man
who watches and celebrates her with his voice. Tree facing blissful tree.
She saw the men go off to war,
was plunged in the war like the first early morning in her memory.
Early morning with bell and broken crickets.
Her heart sinking in the forest.
Like a planet her glimmers, she sent her sons off to war.
You can still make out her glance, while there's one solitary
star, a palm tree. From her hands came naked uniforms,
shirts, and secret flag lights.
She was born for love, she burns in love, sensing the fruit,
for love her waist has grown like the world's edges,
and a deep peace springs from her hair and her dress

pero si siente de la patria el grito
yet if she hears the cry from the homeland

The Sun in the Snow

*The poor poet has died,
and we did not come to know him.*
                                José Martí

The radiant Homeland was in the mute snow
and the suffering Homeland heard wearily the eternal green,
The muscular Homeland listened to a torrent thunder beneath a banished star
and the sickly Homeland drank its cup of Paris grey sky in absinthe.
The enamoured Homeland pulsed darkly in its banishment
and the impotent Homeland in its banishment contemplated the same blue sky upon the same green snow.
The Homeland of banishment twisted its deep tobacco leaf-rooted
and the Homeland banished in itself blindly contemplated fronds' silky murmuring.
And the banished Homeland called to the sun of the earthless Homeland
and the earthless Homeland cried out for banishment's snow.
The living Homeland wanted to melt the dying Homeland in a great sun
did the dying Homeland want to grab hold of the great sun like the handle of an eternal possession?
Father father I'm here close and naked
I all those who've loved you and suffered
and all those who wandered alone
like a defeated army
await the father who must come
to melt me into him in an embrace
perhaps he will also call me
                         son
Father father such a slow weariness
such a strange suffering
it was strange to be alone and strange
not to have a pillow to lie on

or a dream stone
You saw me from a torrent
I waited for you in the snow of a tender wing
raining like a benediction
Together together both below a sky
We grow sour instead of loving one another
I with my tired feet you with the
marble thought of your forehead
We grow invidious instead of making way together
Together the two of them upon the bleeding earth
among red frond and fruit
hiding a foreseen light
Father father such a long path
    I bring them together
I bring them together They embrace

The Homeland was in the snow hearing the torrent thunder
  breathing the cold air drying the delicious palm.
The Homeland took its absinthe star as bleeding host in the hostile
  rundown café.
The Homeland in the snow called to its warriors gathered sweat's
  meager coins.
The Homeland in the fronds listened to vague noises from another
  world vague and grey.
The Homeland dying in the shadow. The Homeland died with its
  face to the sun.
The Homeland waited for the Homeland to come to save it from its
  abyss.

He Has Told Me

He has told me everything is good, Everything,
for something: the infinite stars
shining, and this tiny dark stone
I've picked up, Zampanò, from the mud.

I am like this stone, or like the bottom,
always empty, of a bottle,
shining broken and in the deep mud
responding to the star's smile.

Why don't you throw me, idiot, from the path,
kicking the stone at your whim,
and go with the rest of the women?

What's in your head? The Madman came
in the starry night and has told me...
Zampanò, do you love me? do you love me?

Luis Lorente

Fable Rain

The evening lingers.
On the brevity of excesses it's raining.
The sea doesn't cease and piles up round
the surprise of the angry guest
who came to ask why so much hounding,
so many opposed days for fortune
to half-open doors.
It's raining near everything too much.
On the minority, on the nonconformists,
on the sleepless and the town of defenceless monsters,
on a soul calling out for its face, it's raining still.

How will my children leave here now,
peaceless aunts horrified
before the unexpected and the agony,
permanencies agreed upon by twilights and waves.
Here was always yesterday.
Something came to be embedded out in the open
to swiftly invade what
makes us unreasonably miserable.
Soon once more the evening dead
among occasions and the almond tree's propitious branches
one often says: I still can't explain for how long.
That the world might know you're secluded
and you're going to write letters from the distance.
Not even God knows. Today on everything it's raining.
Passionless Thursdays, packed with innocents,
the effect and its causes, return to what they've been.
I don't trust. I wait. I fashion another house on top of mine.
I resuscitate and if they let me I speak of those who disregard
    the gallows' noose,
of those who've dug their own graves,

of those who don't recall if they have a brother,
if they were born in this or another Milky Way.
All of them fleeting, all usurped, throat filled with holes.
What will become of us all the balconies fallen,
when next year no one has any windows.
Unshakeable with the same custom as dinosaurs.

Will this rain always be tremendously guilty
of me thinking at times I've been buried
and I give up exhausted, distanced from the revelations,
now suddenly made an invariable oblivion,
the past and future of sunrays?
Mine was the fatal, the desire to be, except for myself, any man
who denies and affirms because I'm going to die
so slowly that then my eyes are eaten away
from seeing this rain like a mansion
for the possessed and others condemned.
The prayers won't make it to heaven.
Night has the habit of a guillotine
and we're more or less, different, frightened,
each other, aunts and children, owners of violins,
the memorizers in disagreement with everything they silence.
Tomorrow another slip-up might cost us snow
and the hurricanes to burst like a tongue.

The rain falls on my back, think twice about it it warns me,
don't let it be you who comes to hear what the solitary, undone
spirits dialogue.
Until yesterday the lengthened fringe was a kingdom with
    illusions of grandeur.
Still dormant they always went to that spot to bury the dead,
horizon guarded with extreme caution by
ivory towers and fish dreams.
Who will live after these cities
and the homes perplexed by mold masks
when everyone's become runaway slaves once more,
when surroundings are a cathedral collapsing;
and defeated armies, blown by the wind

now wander over the rubble.
Everything's disfigured, drips, sinks,
becomes an obsession for the angry guest
who has found no one to respond to him.
Of what was once yours, what will become, our father.
What will become of us who remained
and slept quietly while the rain fell
with its swollen fists against the unsustainable,
against the empty flank, the space of a man
who could repeat each night we went
trying to die, helpless, in our beds.

Under the Wheels

Why do the dead want hearts
if they're keeping on barefoot,
stealthily, sunken in a bottle?
Why the need to proclaim themselves, write up manifestos,
raise barricades upon the very shifting sand
if they'll never be able to see or speak or hear?
Why feel hunger when now the sowing
has spread to the hills of dim purgatory?
How is it they're obsessed with knowing their future
if they're only granted what's final?
Why cry out for company if the sentence is irrevocable?
Why ask to see one other, dialogue, make after dinner conversation
if spiders copulate behind their portraits?
Why are arrows so pressing when arrows were what
changed them to eternal poplars and statues?
Why ask for a ceasefire when they don't disagree,
aren't alternatives, don't aspire to power?
Why yearn so for incidences of spring?
What more do the dead want?
What more do they want to know?

José Pérez Olivares

The Magician
(Arcana I)

I'm arriving, finally, to the age where the *sudden decantations of the body, the so very slow fleeings of pleasure* begin.

They say at that age one reaches plenitude in all things, since the latter spin round the mature man opening doors in unison; the doors with their ferocious internal mechanisms.

They say that death is found far off, in its kingdom of serpents, and that life ends up being more translucent after youth's lightning. I have within reach the perfect equation. My life is no longer a hieroglyph written in the wind; stone someone threw to the current's centre. I am half effigy, half human, like the man from the Da Vinci painting, with his legs spread in a signal of defiance. Just like a merchant I've offered little and received double. Facing me the arrogant were ruined; fell like old walls shaken by an earthquake. On the other hand, I've given the world my words (I heard them once more from the mouths of the people, or they were lost swallowed by the night). Sometimes barefoot and shirtless I walked on the grass and went back to my childhood: where *the creature / sees itself in the distance when the distance is named / in the supreme essence and the supreme form*, and we move forward through time with a soft, purple tongue, feeling for the nubile arms of immortality.

I hindered no one, I had no enemies, only melancholy ghosts surround me. That's all. I blow on the flute and suddenly the mice appear.

Reflections by the Painter James Ensor

*Le vulgaire ne discernera que désordre, chaos,
incorrection.*
                                                      J.E.

For the nomadic children
I've painted Christ's Entry into Brussels.
For the indifferent, the bishops and the choir singers
I've painted Christ's Entry into Brussels.
For the desperate
dragging a body beneath the rain,
for miracle workers and suicides
I've painted Christ's Entry into Brussels.
It might seem absurd to paint Christ
surrounded by that riffraff;
it might seem banal
to put my art to function for so much mediocrity.
Without anyone knowing, I took the brush and the colours
and I painted those garish masks,
squeezed a tube of red and a tongue appeared;
made a line at random,
                        and out came, vehemently, a cry.
All day
and the night that follows that day,
and the next morning
I painted and painted unceasing
                            Christ's Entry into Brussels.
Those faces frighten;
there's so much fear in them, so much ugliness;
there's so much dementia in this painting,
and in the middle is Him
and the city of Brussels in the background.
Actually there are no faces, just masks;
city doesn't exist either
just a hell of colours.

I don't know who'll come to contemplate this work.
People, when they see it, will be shocked
and turn their sight from there
like they turn their sight from something indecent.
Actually, it is an indecent painting
for an indecent world.
And everything I've shown
is nothing more that pure indecency.
That's why I titled it
                'Christ's Entry into Brussels.'
Where the horror is, that's where Christ ought to be.
Where the arrogance is, Christ ought to be.
Where the indecency is, Christ too.

I'm calling Christ with my painting.
I'm saying to him, 'Lord, this was the world you created in your image.'

Before the crowds knock down my door
and drag me around like a bundle
and slap me and spit on me
for painting your face among murderers and prostitutes,
I must finish, at last, your triumphal glance in Brussels.

Reflection on the Kiss of Judas

Giotto, Scrovegni Chapel, Padua

Who, at some point, wasn't kissed on the cheek by Judas.
A Judas lying in wait everywhere
and living in all eras.

And who, at some point,
wasn't a little cowardly
and small-minded like Judas.
Who hasn't kiss Christ on the cheek
with a long, thirsty kiss like his.

Soleida Ríos

Flows

2

With Gigi

she comes by a path that is a mountain clearing sometimes I can see her plainly sometimes the shadows of the trees hide her

she comes slowly headless... she carries her head in her arms as if it were a child something to be loved something to care for

---

5

With Cira

I changed to a bird red but big bigger than a peacock and *red red* and I was as if fire and flew at the height of the houses and as I passed by the houses were burning burning burning so and it was in the daytime and you couldn't see the sun

8

With Any

I only see the sea the same dark sea and a thin man with big teeth and green glasses alone in a storm riding in a boat with an oar in his hand as if trying to hold on with the oar to not fall trying for the boat not to tip from the storm's strength... then he looks at me and laughs he always looks at me and laughs

11

With Darsi

everything began with the rain and the thunder I saw the temple of the virgin of el cobre and I saw many people the columns come apart on high and half of the temple leaning forward folks running terrified here and there and there are cries and so much noise and so much confusion

those who came with me and I we felt all that was a warning (I carried a girl by the hand perhaps she was me) the temple once more takes on its original shape whirlwinds of dust upward form and leave great gusts of fire in a dark storm cloud

everything is open air the buildings begin to sway but the earth doesn't move what's ending is the sky

in our hurry to seek shelter those who came with me and I have lost our way

12

With David

it was a theatre walls nothing more but ruined walls and very high windows no partitions no third or fourth floors stunned we look I say this it's going to fall it's going to collapse but we climbed stairs and up top there was no sky only leafless trees I predict this once more it's going to fall and it filled with white black mestizo people smiling dancing and I knew they were going to die...

the theatre fell I grabbed hold of a tree (each window had a tree like a bar a guardian bar salvation) I hung there

there was no sky or world just that swaying tree

Tuesday the 13th in the Sargasso Sea

A.D. Morales

There's a dark stripe yes
it's tar
below the eels spawn
dead fish come to eat from my mouth
this isn't the garden of delights
we aren't going to inaugurate love
we won't invent anything
(perhaps in dreams
we'll embody some turbid prophecy)
we're dirty impure
we live in the Sargasso Sea
the other animals spill their jelly and envelope us
open their rigid tails and the edge slashes the medusas
and envelopes us
and those open eyes say nothing
there's no news
from the far side the dogs barking in a circle
and beyond the wolves howl at the dogs
and the horn of stealthy hunters
grazes their backs
there's no news
we have no news
no future light substitutes or clarifies
this weightless day
these mountains of gleaming garbage
if I open my body so it can be touched by an angel's wand
it's a lie
we eat and turn over demon's meat
I kiss and curse in you the men to come
I kiss and curse those who one day
built me and devastated me
we have no news
these waters are thick pestilent

we are a lone darkened object
we are alone and accompanied like the world
desperate like the world
our bodies are nostalgic for another body
they live with the nostalgia of another time
there's no news
what we do kills us
and whatever we don't do will kill us too
open my body
with that softness unknown to me
invent it now for me
close your eyes
make that sweet fluid linger from another night
from another distant curve
so very far away.

Reina María Rodríguez

Regrets for a White Lamb

I can't free myself of that eye
seeing my imperfections
from the canvas.
all my guilt of living
and loving
making me up.
I'm searching for myself
and I'm frightened
almost a fanatical fear
of having been an incomplete
accomplice
for I also smiled when I wanted to kill.
my lies are dreams
water I did not swim
and this vice
this vice of butterflies
just one day, ceaselessly soaring
then dark blight upon the violets.

forgive me   eye of my young lamb
if in these years I fooled you
and could have been
different.

The Women Write Love Letters

they write until the light turns off
until the tiny flame burns down.
they write in bathrooms   in offices
hidden from teachers and rats.
they write still unresting
to place in the bottom of trunks
little dead things   letters stuck to the paper
the sophistication of words
they wanted to make
some voyage never exact.
they write love letters with preambles
bits of paper placed once and again
in different ways.
thrown from the globe of ingenuity
from the hospital from the castle
where dreams that couldn't linger appear.
with so much fear like descending a wet pedestal
sleepwalking they write
with no other skill than a heart lightly corroded
by the fierce talons of years
by the blue ink petrified in nights of waiting.
they write to convince someone
to convince just one person
who perhaps hasn't come
or has gotten lost definitively
in the crowd.

The Winter Garden Photograph

was always the one we wanted and couldn't have.
the winter garden was near the park
with its wet windows beneath the sun coming through
in the afternoon, or in the morning, to colour its plants.
I walked hand in hand with you – you were
a bit shorter than me –
and so I could see, from that height,
the stems broken by my mother
who formed and trimmed the potted bougainvillea.
we never went in, we were too small
to invade the trusted zone of those strange beings
who remained inside. we were outside.
jumping for no reason with our energy
barred from the patience of my mother's hands
but it's there where I'd like to live...
in the inexact place of a photo that's missing
so I don't imitate once more, or try to imitate the being I am.
the forbidden landscape where we'd put love exclusively.
the landscape of desire, not overlapped or reproduced at each instant,
it stayed hidden for us –
the racket of being children didn't let us see
'we all went around hunting for an insectivorous flora.'
we were suspicious. now, I find a spot in my mind
for the mind of the winter garden. its warm flame
in the middle of images making us believe something shook
or couldn't be reachable.
that uncertainty of the shaking where wood creaks
and reality's distorted and breaks in two languages
was what we always wanted and couldn't have.

9 March 1995

Alex Fleites

Cancelled Poem

Resigned,
the stamps await the light
to be shed Monday
on desks and windows

First will be
to certify the day,
verify that Sunday has passed
with its unhurried alcohol;
Second,
extend Tuesday's visa,
saviour of an order
that knows more
of a woman's curves
than the dizzying spiral

Colossal,
addicted to ink's darknesses,
fans of certainty,
like public employees
they have secret sorrows
often coming
from their wooden hearts
There are days
they'd like to be
a tree once more
– with everything even jays –
Then it's absolute anger
and they mark
CANCELLED
or
YOUR REQUEST
HAS BEEN DENIED

Few know
the resentment of a branch
that could have at least
been a table
for cherished bread,
and in pieces
among paper clips
that know nothing more
than how to talk about the boss

Still,
they too have their joys
Occasions when they give their
SEAL OF APPROVAL
to the home where the man will live,
grant births
and bear witness to battles
with no unfortunate losses

In any case,
and given their bureaucratic sadness,
it's advisable to keep them
out of the hands of children

Simple Story

Slow in its dying,
the fish with a mistaken name
doesn't know I watch it
while the instant arrives
to pay for the scale's gold,
the glassy spheres
now glance at nothing,
the pleasure they stole from the sea

It's so simple the story
horrifying:
it will lose its savage scent
before the cruelness of lemon,
and in the end other will be
its shape and colour
thanks to oil's fire

Small is the fish's tragedy
this morning on the planet,
a winter showing
deaths and farewells and borders;
minimal is its way of going
to revive as impulse
of caress, blow
I'm going with the fish
Someone's looking at me with envy

Víctor Rodríguez Núñez

Prologue – to Rafael Alberti's *The Lost Grove*

When Halley's comet
old bandit of the skies
cut night's belly with its switchblade
my grandmother
               who still wasn't the grandmother
of anyone in this world
dreamed of clean hair
and put six sparrow eggs in her mortar
that became
          who knows how
                 dust enamoured
to reshape her damp face
in the sad way of the moon

Yet in another corner of this planet
spinning like a swarm of wasps
when Halley's comet
put away its switchblade bloodied with night
a boy from Cádiz with bay-like eyes
longed to comb sky's swift hair
with his trident of a sailor on dry land

The century has had
               to pass
                      desperately
night's wounds have scarred
the boy is not the boy
               but an old man
a banished poet returning
the grandmother is not the grandmother
but a bee
        stinging the soul
of another boy who combs in his memory
the clean hair
               of one night in the world

Marco Polo's Dilemma

for Margaret Randall

I've seen something of the world
Managua dust storms
bare snow
covering the pines along the road to Smolyan
and the flags arguing atop the tower
of the University of Puerto Rico

I've seen something of the world
Palenque's bewitched stones
the bay of honey
forgotten by summer at Ponta Delgada
and the Red Square
painted by Kandinsky

I've seen something of the world
and it only deepens my sorrow
Nothing belongs to me

Praise for the Neutrino

for Jesús Selpúveda

I celebrate you
             because no-one in the world
is smaller
        and still
you cross galaxies nebulas stars
not reacting

Because even as light
                 you move
much slower than light
or rest motionless
               correcting
the theory of a warming universe

Because thanks to you
                 the past was only
reheated plasma and not ashes
Plasma's density reached
billions of tons
by cubic centimeter

Because no one knew
                until now
you were ninety-seven percent
of everything
          leaving only three to be divided up
among sons of bitches and the rest

Because thanks to you
                no-one's far
from anyone now and everything tends to join
And it doesn't matter if
in a solid flame
at a radiant point

I celebrate you
                because you are
                              essence of spasm
matter of tenderness
or that tiny bit of nothing
my aunt uses to brown her custards

Thank god
                the world isn't infinite
Like a verse
                it's made up of syllables
that can be counted
The world fits in an alexandrine

Ángel Escobar

A Question

according to you apparently tenderness is sold on ice cream
    cones
and one just goes around licking it as he pleases /
if that's the way it was why does the paper say Adam got his
    lower belly
pierced by a bullet made of corrugated matter
and why has Víctor Jara severed his ear
and why did they tear off Van Gogh's hands in the middle of the
    stadium
when he decided to paint crows the size of the sky

according to you tenderness / then tell me
      why
did they hollow out Pushkin's eyes in the Moncada Barracks
      why
did other inquisitors impale Roque
      why
doesn't Lorca write not even a gentle love poem any more
since they blackened his face this morning
and why so much filth
      why
does a crowd still burn their aspirations
beneath a Bolivian landscape
you say tenderness
when hate leaves our fists red-coloured
you say tenderness / you want me to repeat
      tenderness
but I won't take it back
they can hang me while I cry out
that rage is round and moving

7:15 a.m.

The sun like a ballerina grazes the marble
after breaking into pieces as it crosses the shutters.
It's come to find us, another five and me –
to scratch its back
                        up and down and all along
its ignorance in hospitals. The woman
knows more, the santera in white,
than the sun or the moon. And for example you,
now with no discord,
feel like a young horse in the shade,
and you talk to Juan Clemente Zenea about the sun
and the hay bails you have to haul
at the same schedule – for the fire tanker
trucks,
for the big rats in the market and for
the gymnasts from that old high school nine years
ago.
No one else coughs here. Only the light trips
on my hand.
Only the sun repeats these signs. And comes,
and goes, and stays slipping on the marble –
Missteps.

Sense

I'm fleeing myself like a dream.
Evenings and women hide me
in their wet cells –
which is a lie. I'm exposed,
I'm a deserter of you and I'm afraid.
I could simply write the complacence
of my peers – mine are other reasons.
(On a rock there is no rest;
we could see the sea or a sentence's stone,
that would annul the reason for the sense revealed.)
Not one single tear. I see a vest,
a room with its last spiders.
And where do I wait for you? For the love I knew
distance is missing, my hands are its hands
and there's a knife upon the waters from before.
My anguish is its contentment,
still it's good it gleams –
the ice of my entrails gleams too.
In reason I bury myself, in the dry music.
Ancient I am and my death is uttered.

Ramón Fernández-Larrea

Transitory Poem

to Víctor Rodríguez Núñez

It's hard to live on bridges

Behind remained the black mouth the hate
and not emerging is the splendour
this too is the splendour
but not either

The blinding light will always be up ahead
The blinding light will always
its nest is at the top
toward there go your steps Don't linger
don't linger don't
or the vertigo will sink its tremble into your eyes
the blinding light will always be before you
toward there goes your blood still you won't see it

It's hard to live on bridges.

Reina Street's Arcades

tomorrow will never get here
there is no tomorrow I'm missing a leg
because my leg I've lost it thinking
tomorrow would arrive and they spoke

my leg doesn't grow there was a mine
that never appeared in the reports
there was a mine on the highway and my letter
burned like everything one expects from others
now I stretch out my hand without shaving
now I stretch out my hand beneath the rain placed

by wooden balusters they perch on faces
the dead sky fainting on your belly
a foot
two pairs of shoes
five useless throats
the name of each one of us
knifed beneath their shadow

for twenty-five years I've been seeing
the bitter ones run when the sun's hair is tousled
sitting beneath my cap preserving pieces of night
and I swallow the pieces like lone crusts of bread
I've seen them run behind the fox
undress near the room they pay so much for
smoke swearing and leave their little son
who never stops crying
I've seen them admirable and admired
solid and pompous
sad and at the point of leaving
the galaxy they make at times impossible

the dust lights up and what's different
is the sensation of nullity or the tiger

gets more tired than ever
among the pages of geography
it bleeds preserving its fur

my beautiful life of narrow thighs
the old lady who never knows
where to leave her last money
black men happy like switchblades
pregnant ladies left out and sleepy
ministers of another sky who tarnish
voiceless howlers who become stimulated
poor fellows and child commissioners
hanging from god with four wheels
pretty girls with water up to their necks
who forget the poet's birthday
pigs gnawing at my shirt
the only shirt given to me
by communists with no angels or sword
impossibilities and inscriptions
in hospitals in albumin
audits almost bled dry
with children who sleep storyless
I'm here in the reina arcades
I'm as if no one can glimpse me
I'm skipping over the script of life

and the day lifts
full of dust and recent executioners
who kissed a puffy-eyed woman
she surprises me / opening breast cancer and watching humans run /
and there is / mother/ a great city in the world called paris /
and there's another in reina street's arcades / where you live naked /
or you don't live/
or buy a child's saliva to survive /
or put up posters / that say viva fidel / to sell afterwards
shampoo for fifty pesos / a hopeful oil painting / some cross /
trees at the foot of their orphanage /

or because I
the blind man narrating
the birth of all the worlds
whistling of all the panthers
the murmuring of every ancient wall
broke my sleep like a breastbone
in the second police station
my brother who also makes a face and memory
lost half a violin in his ear
his ear and nobody cares

because the wolves sing in these arcades
the wolves sing and nobody cares
if a violin crackles when it is its moon
because the wolves sing in these arcades
beneath the planks of the past and the year two thousand
leave their shine and the puddles surround
the possibility of the children breathing

the one sitting with diverse foreheads and giant eyes
me the miserable one the dirty one the mutilated one says it
me the one who has no other choice
but to see and see and my punishment
is to see what to see and once more see
beneath my cap in the arcades
me who grew up with a sky in my hand
a defenceless hand called darkness
who glimpses at steps and sexes
me the solitary one
who swallows the evening
me the oarsman lampless pocketless
who stretches out a hand with no answers
when the sun shakes itself dry.

Roberto Méndez

I Can Open My Eyes

I'm going to close my eyes here, sitting in this flowerbed in the middle of the avenue,
it's three in the morning and thousands of photoelectric cells are lit up in all the parks,
what might the girls tousled by a furious wind be doing
on their beds, today, their first night?
How might the lonely old people be sleeping in their homes filled with portraits?
At this hour, how might the jungle be roaring among the seated colossuses of Angkor?
At what point might the battles be there in the depths of Ajanta's friezes?
Many of those sleeping can love me, for others I'm nothing more than a stranger,
if some loved me yesterday and hate me now, it doesn't matter at all;
it's a comfort to think I can open my eyes and the girls will still be tousled
and the old people tossing and turning in bed, the same indifferent stones will carry on in Angkor or Ajanta.
At this hour the world isn't thinking of me, but it exists:
it's comforting that at three in the morning I'm thinking about what a girl might do with the light on, if there are thousands of photoelectric cells
burning in the parks. I'm here with my eyes closed, but if I open them there will still be stars up above and the moon with its frozen canals,
there will be poets too, alongside the stones, dreaming about someone dreaming of them
and when they awaken something will be different.
Early morning is never the same.

The Stellar

> *It's the comedians who work in a sleeping hermitage,*
> *while at their side a painter works the sign [...]*
> *In those ruins there is no roof,*
> *yet the painter makes the most of it*
> *to pinpoint the stellar.*
>   José Lezama Lima

After the ruins there is no room of mirrors,
not even a mirror to place the third tree,
the ruins are only unroofed columns,
the flute crosses freely between them, they have no more faith
than to consider the past like an indivisible water,
what is the place for contemplation?
where to open the door through the exact position?
Two men backs turned can be invisible,
yet the night keeps on pecking at the tablecloths,
grazing the parleys until only leaving
empty hats, masks, an undone dinner;
among the comedians who leave and the painter
pinpointing in a minimal space the star
only the stellar is like a loud laugh;
I cross, cross again the way of the trees,
do you know why a pine is so different from memory?
Beneath its blankets beautiful bodies might be discovered,
if they slipped into the waters every word would be allowed
still the early morning only welcomes its dances
and it quietly reproaches the scarce music,
how much will you give for that stain?
Some broken glass, the mercurial water that fits in a handkerchief.
I repeat for the Deaf Man: all space can be pinpointed in a sign,
the brush rounds its contours with pity and disgust,
between one mirror and another, dawn and angels breakfasting;
sons of men, will you believe in the death announced as a flute?
Faith can only be above the roofless columns,

it's sad to be invisible yet an errant gesture identifies us
and the mask? Upon the hills there's a lightning bolt,
I conclude the parleys, the table is set for the spirits,
what of the mask? Behind the easel begins the labyrinth:
it only sees an abandoned hermitage and the night,
the comedians' laugh is not enough.

Transfiguration

In its capsule of asbestos, Toledo burns in the distance,
it is night, the ether has bloomed into fruit
before the kneeled wayfarer
who can't be kept apart from the evening and its stations.
The landscape will ascend in porcelain's blue touch,
the pilgrims will confront the ashen garment, the face
not hitting upon the exact expression, the arms calling
the body from the air where lovers flee,
books closed, dust on saddlebags
and further up the birds nibbling at the sky's pomegranates.
It is night, Juan de Yepes has lingered
in the very centre of fear and seen open unto him
the enormous edifice of solitude,
no one can uproot him at this instant from the breath
where he sees a torso and its shadow flee down the paths.
Juan de Yepes found his mountain and will ascend before the dawn,
while in his palm he clasps a drop of dew.

Sigfredo Ariel

En C'est Temps La

What we had at hand
– we don't know what –
has wandered at last to the hands of another master

and that face – we don't know which –
appearing and disappearing on the wall
sang something vaguely familiar
like a story taken place
I no longer recall where.

Everything will be ruthless and brittle
like the women in movies
who suddenly turn blind
planting some geraniums

and the husbands return completely unaware
and lead them
by their pathetic waists
toward another and another darkness.

It will all be simple like pretending a little
to have this century for my convenience
before answering: below opening its mouth
the diving tank / your forehead will smash
against the wall a thousand times gone over and familiar.
There won't be time to sow or gather.
This is the time / the same day
for pruning and the same for fallow land.
Monday today, full moon
thick poplars, look
with the bare bones of cattle
put to boil

my mother made detestable soaps
look
there are whitewashed bones
above and below us / smiles a little
tilts her head

now has begun the brief sensation
of our winter
it's late for movies and lazy things
and what we had at hand
– we'll never know what –
at last has wandered to a true master.

(Other) Lost Labours of Love

To not die
I stretch my hand toward the symbols:
a house, a dog, a foreign country.
I beg for him, mix my tongue
with words dictating the symbol
to the acrobatic heart.
Returns he says *returns*.
He listens to the way a thousand times walked
when Cuba receives the blessing
of a trivial air
these evenings at the four corners
East is the same as West
/ the apparently young oblige you
to grow close to the sea and sleep
if by hand comes
sleep to not know
this is left us.

And I make love with lost eyes.
I wander through Troy, through Baghdad
idle every God given morning
stretch out alongside the symbol
digest for him
I belong to him like music:
quarter of earth
where we build one another
desire and I.

Provisions

At other people's tables I ate with youth
nearly ate with happiness and had my wife
in her parents' bed

and one time we had a house, a horse
pulling the carriage in the lit up evenings

a table to divide the bread, just one glass
to drink from, made of clay

this is the potter's wheel, look, the spinning wheel
this rope was used to lower the servant shape
to the root of the well

at other people's tables we clashed
like two pitchers spilling beer

and the fields curdled with rice
and in the swamps enormous herons
hide their young

it's true
you can no longer control those you love.

Juan Carlos Pérez Flores

The Stranger

for Almelio Calderón

Something's going on, they passed by, there will always be a city
opening and closing before your nocturnal animal eyes,
not such a civil animal, not such a friend of Aristotle.
That city isn't on the maps,
no hand in the sky traced the stones of its foundation
yet you've named it and that's enough for it to stay.
That city isn't on the maps or in the greed of others,
hidden it endures, kingdom off limits to mouths and feet.
That city isn't on the maps
and no hand on earth will order its destruction.
Infinite it is and so small it can hold up your air
that fits like a fish or an apple in one of your fissures.
Magical traveler, cloud gleaner, resounding poor box,
the days will be thick curtains standing in the way
of your eyes and the desired body of gifts,
still they'll be helpless against the force of water.
There you'll return, place your body's mast
against the morning glass and it will start to rain,
a cold, slow rain upon your burns.

Page in Homage to the Goliard Poets

My friend the guardian of flocks has returned. He was in one of those miniature towns there are in the country's inland, next to the swamp, where the days' rhythm is slower and nightfall, outside of hate, you can contemplate a sunset, serpent sliding among the waters and plants, and surrender to an infinite oblivion or the night tides, like a devotee surrenders to the arms of a goddess.

If the homeland exists outside the skin, the abysses, the solitude, the vertigo begin. Others from the same chapel, those who once believed to possess a place in the distribution of the figures, return from strange cities, sing such a sad song, today I set them aside.

I linger before the hands of my friend, flexible and clear from having touched the grass growing along the riversides, calling to a ring, I linger before their eyes, celestial gulfs where the woman appears, like a sailboat, her two halves unfurled. My friend's come back from himself. It grows dark. Outside there's a distant shouting. A cup of tea and quite a few words exchanged in the way two monks speak, they can calm the pain. Oh, times when I've wondered if all this poverty might be nothing more than a treasure, what can be found at mirrors' end.

NASA

Beneath lights constantly changing colour / on improvised dance floors / and other permitted amenities / the new breeds of kids dance / like the kids from back then danced before / to the beat of a music that's now a relic / the music is different and the clothes and hairdos are different too / and there are beer cans smashed against the floor / and a scent of strange cigarettes / and in the adjacent blocks the police cars pass by sounding their sirens and squealing their tires / and to the beat of a music that will soon be a relic / like the kids from back then danced before / the new breeds of kids dance / on improvised dance floors / and other permitted amenities / beneath lights constantly changing colour – suddenly a quarrel and the music stops / and the bodies stop / and the poem stops /

Alberto Rodríguez Tosca

Pandemonium of Freedom

On one side of the bars, the prisoner;
on the other, the free man.

A third sitting on the edge of the bars,
'Which one is the prisoner which
is the free man?'

They don't know which one is
the prisoner which the free man either.
They're confused by the bars and the third man
above them who asks once more:
'Which one is the prisoner which
is the free man?'

And later he reveals to them: 'I'm
the third man sitting on the edge of the bars,'
and then: 'The last visit's
over.'

The free man sits.
The prisoner doesn't come to see him again.

Artemisa, 1983

All the Happiness Is in a Telephone Booth

*for Rafael Alcides
this modest prolongation
of his conversations with God*

and all the filth and all
the helplessness.

No better place
to take up the knowledge
of great absences: here
is man alone and not even
the other end is anyone.

I am
the man alone and you are God
and I am once more the man.

There's no difference between your word
and mine, except
our interlocutors are deaf.
There's no difference between your deafness
and mine, except our interlocutors
talk too much.

Stick
your nose in the cloud and say
if I need motives when I waste
time and change emptying
into your wiry beard a bit
of this horror.

Lord,
I don't believe in You, still I ask you
to defend me tonight
from the gods I believe in. Look at them

walking among men disguised
as men.

Recognize them
from their sureness: they are sure.
They go back to streets, clubs, offices
and sureness follows them
like a shadow. And if it rains it acts
as their umbrella and as handkerchief if it's sunny.

They don't need your forgiveness since
'they know what they're doing.' They don't realize
you've abandoned them and so
they don't ask 'My God My God!' It's not
out of pride but ignorance
that they don't ask, Lord.

The earth
still spins to your regret. Tigers
still breath, we land on the moon,
and my mother's heart broke
like an eggshell the most unfair day
of 1993.

I don't blame you for it. At any
rate, one night her youngest son
had to learn to walk wounded
with his eyes open among the crags
smeared with blood, reservoirs
overflowing with snow, and other arduous paths
of your divine Creation.

Wretched the multitudes
who've never entered a telephone
booth. Poor things my God they know
it all: they know each other and they know me
and I'm the man and I don't know myself.

But don't worry, Lord: the city
doesn't know its parents the children
don't know their brothers the brothers
buy alcohol in the suburbs
and get drunk with a crazy boy
who knows everything and is always
silent.

I'm closer to all of that
than the parents than the children than the
brothers and even the crazy boy.
And I get drunk more
and I'm more silent, only now it's
really late to clean the good name
of this wisdom fallen on hard times.

Is it understood that I speak for myself,
that I'm not endangering anyone, that I'm
the man alone and you're God
and that I'm once more the man, lifted
onto two legs and speaking for myself,
after putting up for so many years
with the words of others defining me?

Oh if being the man and God
and being once more the man meant something!
If being here if speaking if resisting silently.
But none of that means anything.
We're wasting time, Lord. I've run out of
change.

Good-bye.

Carlos Augusto Alfonso

Stockholm Syndrome

I'm not captured
because nothing will be given for my head.
I no longer have behavioural disorders;
to go through the door and back,
I'd only want that,
and to not be shielded
from having my legs shot at the end of the street.
I'll never have new laws of flight applied to me.
I hear them delivering their rash judgments,
I have a feeling my iron mask will be taken off,
while my brother, the imposter,
escapes to the border dressed as a king;
while they decide what to do with the hostages,
I ask permission to make like an Indian
climbing to his bed of roses.
Absolved, and in the same conditions,
I get tangled in the wave that buried Atlantis.
I'm with the balseros who repeat the phrase:
'To change course repentantly.'
Today I defend my life with a xenophobia,
with my hands I excavate the remains of the acropolis
and find the vases I've bitten;
the statues that struggled to run,
I've heard them say I was detained,
I enjoyed a few passes with no one noticing;
I watched but didn't seem like I did.
I remind my guardians of the time,
to go with them facing it all.
I aspire only to serve as a shield,
shunning the row of rescuers.
To avoid the torches of the people searching for me,
I order their magicians to make me disappear.

And an alarm doesn't cease in the quarters,
only endemic birds we dirty it all,
we'll leave the cage
holding the head of Hidalgo.
There's something it's telling me

                              they'll tell me to run!

There's something it's telling me

                              I won't be able to move.

With the cage covered
I'm taken before the presence of a third,
he's a 'stop who goes there.'
If I speak I see the door open,
there's no possible exchange,
since I've heard it said
nothing will be given for my head.

The Dog

The doorbell rings
    I'm Pavlov's dog
    who's lost its days and nights
    automatically trying to find what others hunted.

The doorbell rings
    and I try to find myself,
    there's a different smell than the one of their fear,
    there are new homages,
    the fleas no longer bite my spots
    or come out to find me,
    my stroll is in the sorrows.

The doorbell rings
    and those I haven't been deceive me,
    there's a light from above,
    for a hormone flower,
    for the son denied,
    for the asylum bait.

The doorbell rings
    and the playground voices besiege me,
    the current is the choir,
    the actor, it's the hand that feeds me.
    Sooner than later
    the pit musicians practice,
    it's a masterless ceremony,
    another's memory, there's a last day,
    there's a neighbour dog,
    it's an entire country.

The doorbell rings
>	my bacillus laud me,
>	and gustatorily my rage expresses
>	new inhibitions.
>	There's a change of guard,
>	there's a new time,
>	I feel it in my saliva.
>	I stand and I'm taller,
>	I'm no longer given entry
>	since they know I always
>	come back without the stick.

The doorbell rings
>	and I think I'm calling them,
>	wise masturbators,
>	sense for sense.
>	A shock to the head of my old masters,
>	they weren't degenerates,
>	and they know I can smell them.
>	Here comes the zapping,
>	I hear the bowl,
>	I'm going to bite the hand.

A doorbell rings
>	and I think I can't,
>	I try to concentrate,
>	I'll segregate in silence
>	to be what I was:
>	the pilgrim Paul,
>	the pilgrim Paul
>	pursuing a Christian,
>	the pilgrim Paul converted,
>	the pilgrim Paul captured,
>	the pilgrim Pavlov, keeping tabs on the door.

Labarum

Around the second day of washing cars at
the intersection of O and 23, I discerned that to
the vexillum there had been added an
X and a P, code name (chi) and (rho),
corresponding to the monogram of Christ in Greek.
Why should you know that? think the rest
of the carwashers with their isosceles rags hanging from
flagpoles, 'In real life this isn't Rome, if
you were in Rome you wouldn't be shooed away like a wasp.'
Ever since that notable day, I look at who's going
inside, the windshields shine,
and that's it.

Ricardo Alberto Pérez

Critical Essay on My Father's Hands

My father had perfect hands
for applauding at the circus.

More than the tightrope walker,
I liked his fingers dancing
in a folkloric passion.

My father's big finger
was a high piece of land
where I climbed each day.

(Perfume maker).

He came back with his hand bandaged:
the circus no longer made sense to me,
even the politicians' speeches
seemed less consistent.

The Painting Where the Dog Was

The painting where the dog
was
isn't anymore.
A mark's left
on the wall.

The dog
that was
in the painting that's gone
has come back,
tame
and resting.

The Poem's Words

The poem is a circle.
A centripetal force.

A mossy circle,
the words
are at risk
of slipping, staying outside.

This poem
knows:
sockets
Caspian
tertiary
herrings
gudgeons
limits
colonies, mollusks,
are its words,
it learned to stomach them.

Living together
they discovered
Caspian
was a sea cow
bleating loudly.

A tertiary cow
feeding on
herrings
gudgeons
mollusks.

Limitless
it swallowed
almost entire colonies.

A cow sloshing.

Omar Pérez López

Mules and Knights

In the cool, shady choir
where entering isn't exactly a risk
some enter sounding their boots against the uncreaking wood,
calked until its ultimate consequences,
the others see how their wet hair
bristles and curves trying to get to the beat;
in the cool, shady choir
being cynical is as handy as falling in love.
When the tenuous roar of the mechanical hare sounds
and once the abacus sketched on a square of earth,
dry and shiny and efficient for three generations,
we willingly set off on a race, no sweat or javelins
and something like a mist of security protects us and loves us
and we breathe life like an abacus.
In the vortex of cool, shady manipulations
we all keep an eye on each other, we look after one another
seeking complicity or jug of water,
we pass mules or knights, this isn't decided upon by chance,
we pass in the two possible roles for man
patient perhaps like resin.

Breadcrumb Soup

This is glory
and if it isn't, it is its thickest crumbs.
In larva style
remembering practically costs me the future
and still connected to such a crystalline hope,
I let myself get overwhelmed by stations
with all kinds of nostalgia or interference.
And so, rawboned,
searching for its portrait in the country's music
I transcribe society dances, arm wrestling matches
in a glade for all and for the good of all
where my melancholy comes out unaffected,
this is glory or at least its most fragrant sawdust,
but no, no way, this is glory.
I'm translating on plywood boards that weigh the same as a fly
the fullness of a certain kind of memories,
look after then, this repertoire of artisanal mirages
that resist the killing and salting of memory,
lean over and repeat after me: this is glory
and if not one of its most golden peels,
but no, no way, this is glory.

Evangelicals

Those who never lied much or know nothing of the
inaccessibility of truth; with insolence (jovial, divine,
whatever you want to call it) illuminate the face of the sleepy
guards. On a subject such as this it's often ruled 'It's a
lamp,' like someone recounting a knife fight or
describing a juridical vocation or a certain chest
capacity. Yet those referred to here don't know
an ember can persuade the whole fire.

The rice stalk returns to its former position
with the same persistence it was trampled with
not with the same violence.

Not for the old tree awaiting the axe
or for the hagiographer
who enjoys only the lives of those he recounts
or for the minor
who through a practiced orifice in a goat hair
looks on high
was the abdication put in place (and yet).
Not for the stone awaiting parapet
or for one who suffers from claustrophobia in the wasteland
or for the astral eunuch, or for one who copies
with pious inexactitude
a trembling to a bar of wax, was the abdication created
and yet, even for them
a circle was cleared in the grasslands.

Damaris Calderón

A Woman Alone and Bitter

I

When you were beautiful
when your breast was crossed by furious winds
my mother gave birth to me in a sordid room
in an unknown clinic
gaping like a fish
upon her belly was the weight of a cavalry.
Two inexorable women
pruning the bit of sun in the room
they reminded it of its nearness to the two abysses.
My mother was an enclosed hedge
who at one time had her small fountain
a fence
destroyed by dogs and years.
From her worn wood I rise up to the world
from her rotten wood I refashion the cords of my house
and I cannot reach it.
Like the shadow a horseman follows on the plain.

II

Beneath those hands split by horror
made closer by the flame
my head was lodged
fruit waiting to be pecked by birds
those small docile animals
we couldn't watch without disgust
moving among the plates
when she set life aside for us
for herself.
I came out from between her legs
like a bombing.
I have been hero and traitor.

Mezcal

At the bottom
of a bottle
of mezcal
– like at the end –
waiting for us
is the worm.
I chew
in dry earth
that whiteness
of living hedgerows
to know
the taste
of what will eat me.

Syllables. Ecce Homo

To speak of the babbling bird
blabbermouth balancing on a branch
singing (like Juan Luis Martínez would say)
in birdwords.
And man is a tombstone
a dark room, an empty chair
and a lamp.
He who grows closer to the lamp
can find a way out
(or the illusion of a way out).
Is there a possible way out
or is every way out in,
toward the kingdom of the root?
To sink like Virginia Woolf
with her pockets full of stones in the river.
Here is the true profit.
What surface swimmers don't reach.

Optimism is a flag at half-mast
yet flaunted with joy.
A consolation or a self-consolation,
'I rose from my cadaver and went in search of who I am.'

Like the surgeon cuts,
the syllables break apart.
Flesh of the scission,
scission of the flesh.

A bird came with its head bandaged
a splinter from the third world war
Apollinaire singing in a cage
Ezra Pound's golden tetradrachms.

Like the hare in the grove,
word in language.
Anguish jumps the perimeter
and starts to run about the rooftops.

Biographies

Fina García-Marruz
Havana 1923. Poet, essayist, and literary critic. Doctor in Social Sciences from the University of Havana. She formed a part of the group of poets who edited the journals *Clavileño* (1942-1943) and *Orígenes* (1944-1956). From 1962 to 1987 she was a researcher at the National Library in the Centre for Studies on José Martí. Cuba's National Literature Prize (1990), Chile's Pablo Neruda Prize (2007), Spain's Reina Sofía Prize for Ibero-American Poetry (2011), among other honours. Poetry: *Poemas* (1942), *Transfiguración de Jesús en el Monte* (1947), *Las miradas perdidas: 1944-1950* (1951), *Visitaciones* (1970), *Poesías escogidas* (1984), *Viaje a Nicaragua* (1987, with Cintio Vitier), *Créditos de Charlot* (1990), *Los Rembrandt de L'Hermitage* (1992), *Viejas melodías* (1993), *Nociones elementales y algunas elegías* (1994), *La anunciación* (1995), *Habana del centro* (1997), *Antología poética* (1997, prologue by Jorge Luis Arcos), *Poesías escogidas* (2000), and *Obra poética* (2008, two volumes, prologue by Enrique Saínz). García-Marruz is today's leading figure in Cuban poetry, where she has left a profound mark with her fertile talent and intellectual rigor. With complete stylistic freedom, she breaks free of the speculation of *Orígenes* to draw closer to the quotidian, melding high and popular cultures and offering an inclusive construction of the Cuban nation. Her work lays the foundation for the dialogic poetry that has prevailed in Cuba since the fifties.

Carilda Oliver Labra
Matanzas 1924. Poet and prose writer. Doctor in Civil Law from the University of Havana. She worked as a lawyer, a librarian, an art instructor, and a middle school teacher. Among other honours, Cuba's National Literature Prize (1997) and Mexico's José Vasconcelos Prize (2002). Poetry: *Preludio lírico* (1943), *Al sur de mi garganta* (1949, 1990 and 1994, National Poetry Prize), *Biografía lírica de Sor Juana Inés de la Cruz* (1951), *Libreta de recién casada* (1952), *Canto a Martí* (1953), *Memoria de la fiebre* (1958), *Antología de versos de amor* (1963), *Tú eres mañana* (1979, July 26th Décima Prize), *Las sílabas y el tiempo* (1983), *Desaparece el polvo* (1984), *Calzada de Tirry 81* (1987 and 1993, anthology, prologue by Rafael Alcides Pérez), *Los huesos alumbrados* (1988), *Sonetos* (1990), *Se me ha perdido un hombre*

(1991), *Ver la palma abriendo el día* (1991), *Antología poética* (1993 and 1997, prologue by Marilyn Bobes), *Noche para dejarla en testamento* (1996), *Discurso de Eva* (1997), *Libreta de la recién casada* (1998), *Sombra seré que no dama* (2000, anthology), *Error de magia* (2000, anthology, prologue by Virgilio López Lemus), *Prometida al fuego* (2002, anthology), and *Antología personal* (2004). Among contemporary Cuban poets, Oliver Labra has achieved great popularity and critical praise as a forerunner of poetry that breaks with solipsism and develops a gender consciousness.

Lorenzo García Vega

Jagüey Grande, Matanzas, 1926 – Miami, USA, 2012. Poet, prose writer, and essayist. He studied Law, Philosophy, and Letters at the University of Havana. He formed a part of the literary group *Orígenes*, an experience he recounts in *Los años de Orígenes* (1978 and 2007) and *El oficio de perder* (2004). Exiled since the sixties in both Spain and the United States, he worked at a number of different jobs, including as a bag boy at a supermarket. Poetry: *Suite para la espera* (1948), *Ritmos acribillados* (1972), *Fantasma juega al juego* (1978), *Bicoca a pique* (1989), *Poemas para penúltima vez: 1948-1989* (1991), *Variaciones a como veredicto para sol de otras dudas: Fragmento de una Construcción 1936* (1993), *Caminandito hasta estar sentado* (1999), *Palíndromo en otra cerradura: Homenaje a Duchamp* (1999), *Textilandia albina* (2004), *Vilis* (1998), *No mueras sin laberinto: Poemas, 1998-2004* (2005, anthology, prologue by Liliana García Carril), and *Lo que voy siendo: Antología poética* (2008, prologue by Enrique Saínz). García Vega radically breaks with the central tenets of *Orígenes*, though in a highly personal way, and never turns toward the conversational. From book to book his original neo-baroque style diminishes and more attention is paid to the quotidian, even resorting to anecdote, communication intensifies, and neo-vanguardism is stressed. García Vega's work has not had the wide circulation it merits in Cuba.

Roberto Friol

Havana 1928 – 2010. Poet, prose writer, essayist, literary researcher, and translator. He graduated with a teaching degree in English and studied Medicine for four years, which he abandoned for economic reasons. He taught in elementary, middle, and high schools between 1954 and 1962. Later he worked as a literary researcher at the José

Martí National Library until he retired. After decades of marginalization – he was excluded from the main anthology of his contemporaries, *La Generación de los años 50* (1984) – at the end of his life he received numerous honours: the Fernando Ortiz Medal (1987), Distinction for National Culture (1991), the National Literature Prize (1998), the José Martí National Library Medal (2000), and the Alejo Carpentier Order (2000). Poetry: *Alción al fuego* (1968), *Turbión* (1988, Critics' Prize), *Gorgoneión* (1991, Critics' Prize), *Kid Chocolate* (1991), *Tres* (1993), *Tramontana* (1997, Critics' Prize), and *Zodiakos* (1999, personal anthology). Friol's poetry isn't affiliated with the colloquialism prevalent in his generation, but he does close ranks with García-Marruz in the defence of the small and modest, in the decided solidarity with the other. His is a rigorous exercise in synthesis, mostly based on suggestion, appealing to an apparent expressive simplicity, and requiring at every moment an active reader.

Francisco de Oraá
Havana 1929-2010. Poet, prose writer, literary critic, children's writer, editor, and translator. Still a teen he collaborated with the magazine *El País Gráfico*. At the beginning of the sixties, he was a librarian and professor at the School for Art Instructors and from 1966 to 1996 he was Deputy Editor of the literary journal *Unión*. Awarded the National Literature Prize in 1993, among other honours. Poetry: *Es necesario* (1964), *Celebraciones con un aire antiguo* (1965), *Por nefas* (1966), *Con figura de gente y en uso de razón* 1968), *Bodegón de las llamas* (1978, anthology), *Ciudad ciudad* (1979, Julián del Casal Prize), *Desde la última estación* (1982, anthology), *Haz una casa para todos* (1986, Critics' Prize), *Bodas* (1989), *Mundo mondo* (1989, poems for children, La Rosa Blanca Prize), *La rosa en la ceniza* (1990, anthology, prologue by Enrique Saínz), *A la nada que actúa* (2000, prologue by Mario Martínez Sobrino), *Noche y fulgor* (2002, anthology), and *Figurantes* (2008). In a decidedly personal way, Oraá's poetry synthesizes the poetics of *Orígenes* and colloquialism. It stands out for its wide thematic and stylistic register, where the image is an undeniable means of expression, and clarity and hermeticism mix. Above all, it radically overcomes solipsism. Its poetic subject moves from solitary to solidary, discovers his lineage in others, and instead of differentiating, identifies.

Pablo Armando Fernández
Central Delicias, Holguin, 1930. Poet, prose writer, essayist, screenwriter, and translator. He lived in the United States as a youth and took classes at Columbia University. He returned to Cuba in 1959. He was Assistant Director of the cultural supplement *Lunes de revolución*, Deputy Editor of the journal *Casa de las Américas*, and Cultural Attaché for the Cuban Embassy in Great Britain. As a consequence of the so-called 'Padilla Affair,' he was marginalized. Later he directed the literary journal *Unión*. He is a member of the Cuban Academy of Language, and a winner of the Félix Varela Order in the First Degree (1987) and the National Literature Prize (1996). Poetry: *Salterio y lamentación* (1953), *Nuevos poemas* (1956, prologue by Eugenio Florit), *Toda la poesía* (1961 and 1962, prologue by Ezequiel Martínez Estrada), *Himnos* (l962), *El libro de los héroes* (1964), *Un sitio permanente* (1969), *Suite para Maruja* (1978), *Aprendiendo a morir* (1983), *Campo de amor y de batalla* (1984, Critics' Prize), *El sueño, la razón: 1948-1983* (1988, anthology), *Ronda de encantamiento* (1990), *Libro de la vida* (1997), *En otra estrella* (1998), *Tiempo recobrado* (1998), *De piedras y palabras* (1999), *El pequeño cuaderno de Manila Hartman: 1947-1951* (2000), *Reinos de la aurora* (2001), *Hoy, la hoguera* (2001), and *Órbita de Pablo Armando Fernández* (2003). Fernández is one of the central voices of lyrical colloquialism, he understands poetry as witness, and his language is at times neo-baroque with biblical tones.

Fayad Jamís
Ojocaliente, Zacatecas, Mexico, 1930-Havana, 1988. Poet, visual artist, journalist, translator, and editor. A graduate of the San Alejandro Academy of Fine Arts. In 1954 he moved to Paris where he took on menial jobs and wrote and painted frenetically. Upon returning to Cuba in 1959, along with Fernández Retamar he compiled and introduced the anthology, *Poesía joven de Cuba*, which defined his generation. He was co-editor of the publisher La Tertulia and editor of F. J.; in charge of the cultural supplement *Hoy Domingo*; professor of painting at the National School of Art, and Cultural Attaché for the Cuban Embassy in Mexico. Poetry: *Brújula* (1949), *Alumbran. Seco sábado* (1954), *Los párpados y el polvo* (1954 and 1981), *Vagabundo del alba* (1959), *Cuatro poemas en China* (1961), *Los puentes* (1962, 1981, and 1989), *La pedrada* (1962 and 1972), *Por esta libertad* (1962 and 1977, Casa de las Américas Prize), *La victoria de Playa Girón*

(1964), *Cuerpos* (1966, anthology, prologue by Fernández Retamar and epilogue by Roque Dalton), *Abrí la verja de hierro* (1973), *Breve historia del mundo* (1980, anthology), *La pedrada* (1981, anthology, prologue by Rafael Hernández), *La pedrada* (1985, prologue by Víctor Casaus), *Poemas* (1990, anthology), *Entre la muerte y el alba* (1994, anthology), and *Historia de un hombre* (1995, anthology, prologue by Enrique Saínz). Jamís is one of the most read and influential Cuban poets and his work, decolonizing for its content and decolonized for its form, constitutes a model of dialogic poetry.

Roberto Fernández Retamar

Havana, 1930. Poet, essayist, literary critic, editor, university professor. He received his doctorate from the University of Havana, where he has been a professor since 1962. He became known in the literary magazine *Orígenes*. Since 1965 he has directed the journal *Casa de las Américas*, and beginning in 1986, the entire institution. Among other honours he has received the Félix Varela Order (1981), the National Literature Prize (1989), the Order of Arts and Letters (1994, France), and the May Order (1998, Argentina). Poetry: *Elegía como un himno* (1950), *Patrias* (1952, National Poetry Prize), *Alabanzas, conversaciones* (1955), *Vuelta de la antigua esperanza* (1959), *En su lugar, la poesía* (1961), *Con las mismas manos: 1949-1962* (1962, anthology), *Historia antigua* (1964), *Poesía reunida: 1948-1965* (1966, anthology), *Buena suerte viviendo* (1967), *Que veremos arder* (1970), *Cuaderno paralelo* (1973), *Circunstancia de poesía* (1977), *Juana y otros poemas personales* (1981, Rubén Darío Prize), *Hacia la nueva* (1989), *Mi hija mayor va a Buenos Aires* (1993), *Las cosas del corazón* (1994), *Cuando un poeta muere* (1994), *Aquí* (1995 and 1996, Pérez Bonalde Prize), *Una salva por el porvenir* (1995), *Versos* (1999, anthology), *Esta especie de poema* (1999), and *Órbita de Roberto Fernández Retamar* (2001, anthology). Fernández Retamar is perhaps the most classic example of colloquialism, with his lyric open to reality, his expressive simplicity rich in complexities, with his direct, precise poetic language.

Heberto Padilla

Puerta de Golpe, Pinar del Río, 1932-Auburn, Alabama, USA, 2000. Poet, prose writer, university professor, and journalist. He studied Law and Philosophy at the University of Havana. He lived in the United States between 1956 and 1959, and as a result of the Revolution's triumph returned to Cuba. He was a founding member and leader of the Union of Writers and Artists (UNEAC), a correspondent in the USSR, and an official of the Ministry of Foreign Commerce. In 1966 he was ideologically questioned in *Verde Oliva*, the publication of the Revolutionary Armed Forces. Nonetheless, in 1968 he received the Julián del Casal Prize with his collection *Fuera del juego*. The controversy surrounding the book did not impede its being published, with a note of protest from the UNEAC and another endorsed by the jury. On March 20, 1971 he was arrested; days later he was released and made a humiliating public guilty plea. In the following decade he was marginalized. He left the country in 1980 and lived in New York, Washington, Madrid, and Princeton, where he founded the literary magazine *Linden Lane Magazine*. He taught at various American universities. Poetry: *Las rosas audaces* (1948), *El justo tiempo humano* (1962), *La hora* (1965), *Fuera del juego* (1968, 1971, and 1979, Julián del Casal Prize), *Provocaciones* (1973), *El hombre junto al mar* (1981), and *Un puente, una casa de piedra* (1998). It's unfortunate the 'Padilla Affair' has received more attention than his admirable dialogic poetry, whose language of common exchanges expresses its inconformity with reality.

César López

Santiago de Cuba, 1933. Poet, prose writer, essayist, literary and theatre critic, and translator. Doctor in Medicine from the University of Salamanca, he also studied Philosophy and Letters at various universities. He collaborated with the literary magazine *Ciclón*. After 1959 he was the Cuban Consul in Glasgow and a leader of the UNEAC. During the seventies he was marginalized. He received the National Literature Prize in 1999 and is a member of the Cuban Academy of Language since 1996. Poetry: *Silencio en voz de muerte* (1963), *Apuntes para un pequeño viaje* (1965), *Primer libro de la ciudad* (1967), *La búsqueda y su signo* (1971 and 1989), *Segundo libro de la ciudad* (1971 and 1989, Ocnos Prize and the Critics' Prize), *Quiebra de la perfección* (1982), *Ceremonias y ceremoniales* (1988, Critics' Prize), *Consideraciones: Algunas elegías* (1990 and 1993), *Tercer libro de la ciudad* (1997 and 1998, Critics' Prize), *Libro de la ciudad* (2001, anthology), and *Paisaje, panorama* (2007). López's work is a frank reaction to *Orígenes*, but diverges from colloquialism in its *culteranismo* in both content and form. It is widely receptive to history, politics, and ideology in a more explicit way than most of Cuba's social poets. The poetic discourse registers variations and appeals to tropological language, as in *Quiebra de la perfección*, where the minute and the simple are exalted, and in *Ceremonia y ceremoniales*, where allegory and irony are appealed to.

Rafael Alcides Pérez

Barrancas, Granma, 1933. Poet, prose writer, essayist, and journalist. He studied Industrial Chemistry at Havana's School of Arts and Trades. Before 1959, he was a master baker, farmer, sugarcane cutter, logger, crew cook, sales assistant and store supervisor, mason, housepainter, fumigator, insurance agent, and walking salesman. After 1959, he was an official of the Ministry of Foreign Relations and a founding member of the UNEAC. He stands out as a radio producer, director and writer; for many years he made Cuban poets known with his program on *Radio Progeso*, *En su lugar la poesía*. Since 1993, he has distanced himself from all editorial and public activity, renouncing the UNEAC and writing journalism critical of the Cuban government. Poetry: *Himnos de montaña* (1961), *Gitana* (l962), *La pata de palo* (1967), *Agradecido como un perro* (1983, Critics' Prize), *Y se mueren, y vuelven, y se mueren* (1988), *Noche en el recuerdo* (1989), *Nadie* (1993), and *GMT: Poesía seleccionada, 1963-2008* (2009, anthology). The work of Alcides Pérez, neo-realist, neo-romantic, and always critical of reality, is at the very heart of colloquial poetry. Markedly anti-conventional, he sheds all tropological devices, appeals to narrative and humor, adds a pinch of imagination, and puts everything on the line with a human force, while upholding a notable capacity for communication.

Antón Arrufat

Santiago de Cuba, 1935. Poet, playwright, prose writer, essayist, literary critic, editor, and journalist. A graduate of Philology from the University of Havana. From 1957 to 1959 he lived in the United States and returned to Cuba with the triumph of the Revolution. He became known as a writer in the pages of the journal *Ciclón*. He was a writer for *Lunes de Revolución* and Chief Editor of the journal *Casa de las Américas*. Later he worked as a literary consultant for the Estudio Theatre. He was accused of being a counter-revolutionary for his play *Los siete contra Tebas* (1968, José Antonio Ramos Prize) and suffered more than a decade of ostracism. In the eighties and nineties he wrote for the magazine *Revolución y Cultura*, where he published cultural journalism of a very high quality. He is the recipient of the National

Literature Prize (2000) as well as the Distinction for Cuban Culture and the Alejo Carpentier Medal, among other honours. Poetry: *En claro* (1962), *Repaso final* (1963), *Escrito en las puertas* (1967), *La huella en la arena* (1986, 2000, and 2001), *Lirios sobre un fondo de espadas* (1995, Critics' Prize), *Celari navis y otros poemas* (1996), *El viejo carpintero* (1999), and *Antología personal* (2001). Arrufat's poetry, which denies the orthodoxy of *Orígenes* and affirms the heterodoxy of Virgilio Piñera, is dialogic at its core. Its foundation is a dialectical vision of life, stripped of transcendentalism, and identification with otherness, which is opposed to all exclusionary social norms.

Manuel Díaz Martínez
Santa Clara, 1936. Poet, prose writer, literary critic, and journalist. He studied at the Institute for Hispanic Studies at the University of Paris. He was the Cultural Attaché for the Cuban Embassy in Bulgaria; professor at the School for Art Instructors; Chief Editor of the cultural supplement *Hoy Domingo* and the literary magazine *La Gaceta de Cuba*; researcher at the Cuban Institute of Literature and Linguistics; and scriptwriter and director of programs for *Radio Enciclopedia*. For his connection to the 'Padilla Affair' he was marginalized during the seventies. He was the organizer of the so-called 'Letter from the Intellectuals' that, in 1991, called for changes in Cuban society. Exiled since 1992, he settled in Spain, where he ran the journal *Encuentro de la Cultura Cubana*. Poetry: *Frutos dispersos* (1956), *Soledad y otros temas* (1957), *El amor como ella* (1961), *Los caminos* (1962), *Nanas del caminante* (1963), *El país de Ofelia* (1965), *La tierra de Saúd* (1967), *Vivir es eso* (1968, Julián del Casal Prize), *Poesía inconclusa* (1985, anthology), *Mientras traza su curva el pez de fuego* (1985), *Escritos al amanecer* (1988), *El carro de los mortales* (1988), *Alcándara* (1991, anthology, prologue by Virgilio López Lemus), *Memorias para el invierno* (1995, City of Las Palmas de Gran Canaria Prize), *Señales de vida: 1968-1998* (1998, anthology), *Paso a nivel* (2005), and *Un caracol en su camino* (2003 and 2005, anthology). Díaz Martínez's poetry, unorthodox in relation to colloquialism, does not participate in the neo-realism of the quotidian and at its best moments breaks with solipsism.

José Kozer
Havana, 1940. Poet, literary critic, and university professor. Son of a family of Czech and Polish Jews, he immigrated to the United States in 1960 and settled in New York. There he finished his studies, and from 1965 to 1997 taught Hispanic Literature at Queens College. He spent a few years in Torrox, Spain and since 1999 resides in Miami. Poetry: *Padres y otras profesiones* (1972), *Poemas de Guadalupe* (1973), *De Chepén a La Habana* (1973), *Este judío de números y letras* (1975), *Y así tomaron posesión en las ciudades* (1978), *La rueca de los semblantes* (1980), *Jarrón de las abreviaturas* (1980), *Antología breve* (1981), *Bajo este cien* (1983), *La garza sin sombra* (1985), *Díptico de la restitución* (1986), *El carrillón de los muertos* (1987), *Carece de causa* (1988), *De donde oscilan los seres en sus proporciones* (1990), *Prójimos-Intimates* (1990), *Una índole* (1993), *Trazas del lirondo* (1993), *José Kozer* (1993), *A Caná* (1995), *Et mutabile* (1995), *Los paréntesis* (1995), *AAA1144* (1997), *La maquinaria ilimitada* (1996 and 1998), *Réplicas* (1998), *Dípticos* (1998), *Mezcla para dos tiempos* (1999), *Al traste* (1999), *Farándula* (1999), and *No buscan reflejarse: Antología poética* (2001, prologue by Jorge Luis Arcos). Kozer achieves one of the most radical ruptures in contemporary Cuban poetry. In his work, Jewish culture, Eastern philosophies, his childhood and adolescence in Cuba, the American experience, Lezamian baroque, and a preoccupation with language, all intersect. This poetry, while generally considered to be neo-baroque, actually rejects any stylistic category.

Miguel Barnet
Havana, 1940. Poet, prose writer, author of *testimonios*, essayist, editor, and translator. He studied Advertising and Social Sciences at the University of Havana. He was a professor of Folklore at the School for Art Instructors, a researcher at the Institute of Ethnology at the Academy of Sciences and at the National Library, a consultant for the National Council on Culture, and a writer for the journal *Unión*. He suffered marginalization in the seventies. Later, he founded and directed the Fernando Ortiz Foundation, was the ambassador for Cuba before the UNESCO and a representative of the National Assembly, and currently he is the president of the UNEAC. He has received the National Literature Prize (1994), the International Trieste Prize (2005), and the International Camaiore Prize (2006), among other honours. Poetry: *La piedrafina y el pavorreal* (1963), *Isla de güijes* (1964), *La sagrada familia* (1967), *Orikis y otros poemas* (1980), *Carta*

de noche (1983), *Viendo mi vida pasar* (1987, anthology with new poems), *Claves para Rita Montaner* (1987), *Mapa del tiempo* (1989), *Poemas chinos* (1993), *Con pies de gato* (1993, anthology, prologue by Frank Padrón Nodarse), *Actas del final* (2000), *Cuaderno de París* (2003), *Vestido de fantasma* (2006), and *Itinerario inconcluso* (2007, anthology, prologue by Gaetano Longo). Barnet is the visionary of the generation that comes to be known after 1959, one of the most studied in Cuban literature. His work is not affiliated with anti-poetry, but rather affirms lyrical colloquialism and is radically opposed to solipsism.

Luis Rogelio Nogueras

Havana, 1944-1985. Poet, prose writer, literary critic, screenwriter, and cartoonist. He was a writer for the magazine *Cuba Internacional*, one of the founders of the cultural magazine *El Caimán Barbudo* (1966), and Chief Editor of the journal *Cine Cubano*. He suffered more than a decade of ostracism. Poetry: *Cabeza de zanahoria* (1967, David Prize), *Las quince mil vidas del caminante* (1977), *Café de noche* (1980), *Imitación de la vida* (1981, Casa de las Américas Prize), *El último caso del inspector* (1983), *Nada del otro mundo* (1988, anthology with new poems), *Las formas de las cosas que vendrán* (1989), *Hay muchos modos de jugar* (1990), *Las palabras vuelven* (1994), *Encicloferia* (1999, anthology, prologue by Guillermo Rodríguez Rivera), *Hay muchos modos de jugar* (2005, anthology, prologue by Rodríguez Rivera), and *Hay muchos modos de jugar: Antología poética* (n/d, anthology, prologue by Jesús García Sánchez). Nogueras' work is as much a part of the rise of conversational poetry in Cuba as of getting past it. On the one hand, he develops an existential, confidential, testimonial poetics, on the other, an imaginative poetics, one of intelligence, of intellectual heroism. From beginning to end, Nogueras' poetry is dialogic, since the poetic subject splits into two, into multiple others.

Nancy Morejón

Havana, 1944. Poet, essayist, literary researcher, editor, literary and theatre critic, author of *testimonios*, journalist, translator, and cultural promoter. She graduated in French Language and Literature from the University of Havana. She was associated with the publisher Ediciones El Puente, and Reinaldo García Ramos and Ana María Simo included her work in the first anthology of her generation, *Novísima poesía cubana* (1962). She worked as a writer for the cultural magazine *La Gaceta de Cuba* and directed the Centre for Cuban Studies at the Casa de las Américas. She is an official of the UNEAC and a member of the Cuban Academy of Language. Among other honours, she has received the National Literature Prize (2001) and the Struga International Poetry Festival's Golden Wreath (2006). Poetry: *Mutismos* (1962), *Amor, ciudad atribuida* (1964), *Richard trajo su flauta y otros argumentos* (1967 and 1999), *Parajes de una época* (1979), *Poemas* (1980, anthology, prologue by Efraín Huerta), *Elogio de la danza* (1982), *Octubre imprescindible* (1982), *Cuaderno de Granada* (1984), *Piedra pulida* (1986, Critics' Prize), *Dos poemas* (1990), *Verso a verso* (1986), *Baladas para un sueño* (1991), *Paisaje célebre* (1993), *El río de Martín Pérez y otros poemas* (1996, anthology), *Elogio y paisaje* (1996, Critics' Prize), *Botella al mar* (1996, anthology), *Richard trajo su flauta y otros poemas* (1999, anthology), *La Quinta de los Molinos* (2000, Critics' Prize), and *Cuerda veloz: Antología poética, 1962-1992* (anthology). Morejón's poetry is resolutely dialogic, with an elevated awareness of class, ethnicity, and gender.

Raúl Rivero
Morón, Ciego de Ávila, 1945. Poet and journalist. A graduate of Journalism from the University of Havana. He worked for the news agency Prensa Latina and was Chief Correspondent in Moscow between 1973 and 1976. Later he held senior positions at the UNEAC. In 1989 he abandoned the organization, and in 1991 was one of the signers of the 'Letter from the Intellectuals,' which asks for reforms on the island. In 1995 he founded the news agency Cuba Press, which openly opposed the Cuban government. In March 2003 he was arrested, tried, and sentenced to twenty years in prison, for 'acts against the independence and territorial integrity of the State.' He was freed in November 2004 and since then resides in Spain, where he continues his journalistic work. Among other honours he has received the Maria Moors Cabot International Award in Journalism from Columbia University (1999) and the UNESCO-Guillermo Cano World Press Freedom Prize (2004). Poetry: *Papel de hombre* (1969), *Poesía sobre la tierra* (1972, Julián del Casal Prize), *Cierta poesía* (1981, 26 de Julio Prize), *Corazón que ofrecer* (1981), *Poesía pública* (1983), *Escribo de memoria* (1987, anthology and unpublished book), *Poesía IV* (1988), *Firmado en La Habana* (1996), *Herejías elegidas* (1998, anthology, prologue by José Prats Sariol), *Puente de guitarra* (2002),

and *Vidas y oficios: Los poemas de la cárcel* (2006). Rivero's is an example of participative poetry, in its anti-poetic variant, the trend at the heart of his generation.

Lina de Feria
Santiago de Cuba, 1945. Poet, playwright, children's writer, journalist, and radio scriptwriter. She studied Philology at the University of Havana. She worked in the area of children's theatre for the National Council on Culture; was Chief Editor of the cultural journal *El Caimán Barbudo* (1968-1971); and wrote scripts for programs for *Radio Enciclopedia*. During the seventies she was marginalized. She has received the Rubén Martínez Villena Prize (1965) and the Raúl Hernández Novás Prize (1999), among other honours. Poetry: *Vocecita del alba* (1961), *Casa que no existía* (1967, David Prize), *Lo que va dictando el fuego* (1989), *A mansalva de los años* (1990, Critics' Prize), *Espiral en tierra* (1991), *El ojo milenario* (1995, Critics' Prize), *Los rituales del inocente* (1996, Critics' Prize), *A la llegada del delfín* (1998, Critics' Prize), *El mar de las invenciones* (1999), *El libro de los equívocos* (2001), *El rostro equidistante* (2001), and *Antología boreal* (2007, prologue by Arturo Arango). The work of de Feria does not side with the anti-poetry her generation is known for nor with the colloquialism of the previous generation. In a very personal way, it takes on contradictory forms of expression, and on occasion is a reflection on existence, a vision far from all logic, and on others, a positioning in the quotidian. It is always dialogic poetry since the poetic subject maintains a self-critical attitude and its oscillations in meaning require an active reader.

Raúl Hernández Novás
Havana, 1948-1993. Poet, essayist, researcher, and literary critic. He graduated in Hispanic Language and Literature from the University of Havana. From 1973 until his death he worked at the Centre for Literary Research at the Casa de las Américas. He was awarded the José Lezama Lima Prize in 2000, among other honours. Poetry: *Da capo* (1982), *Enigma de las aguas* (1983, 13 de Marzo Prize, prologue by Cintio Vitier), *Los ríos de la mañana* (1984), *Embajador en el horizonte* (1984), *Animal civil* (1987, Julián del Casal Prize and Critics' Prize), *Al más cercano amigo* (1987), *Sonetos a Gelsomina* (1991), *Atlas salta* (1994), *Material de Lectura de Raúl Hernández Novás* (1996), *Amnios* (1998, anthology, prologue by Jorge Luis Arcos), and *Poesía* (2002, prologue by Arcos). Hernández Novás is one of the leaders of

renovations in Cuban poetry that came about in the eighties. His championing of change can be summed up in his declaration that poetry has to sing, not just converse. To achieve this, he sought a synthesis of different currents of Cuban poetry, though without rejecting colloquialism. It's worthwhile to highlight his wealth of expressive and tropological devices, his use of intertextuality, and his always symbolic language. The poetry of Hernández Novás is no less participative than that of his predecessors, it's based on a materialist and dialectic worldview, and includes both individual turmoil and a heightened social consciousness.

Luis Lorente
Cárdenas, Matanzas, 1948. Poet and editor. Among other distinctions he has received *El Caimán Barbudo* Poetry Prize. Poetry: *Las puertas y los pasos* (1975, David Prize), *Café nocturno* (1984), *Ella canta en La Habana* (1985), *Como la noche incierta* (1991, with Aramís Quintero), *Aquí fue siempre ayer* (1997), *Esta tarde llegando la noche* (2004, Casa de las Américas Prize and Critics' Prize), *Más horribles que yo* (2006, Critics' Prize), and *Fábula lluvia* (2007, anthology). Lorente is one of the first poets to react against the mediocre Socialist Realist poetry Cuban cultural authorities promoted in the seventies, during the so-called Five Grey Years, in an attempt to compensate for the silencing of many of the best Cuban poets of the moment. And yet, this rejection was also aimed at the anti-poetry of the early generation too, that of Ediciones El Puente-*El Caimán Barbudo*, for its prosaicism and its facileness. There is not, however, a return to solipsism, to the individual solution to social problems, since this discourse, capable of notable reflectiveness, is always inclusive. Though never making evident his transgressive will, Lorente enriches dialogic poetry with his lyricism, the elevated tropological density of his discourse, with a musicality not based on metric regularities or an appeal to traditional stanzas, the care he takes with each verse, and his stylized language.

José Pérez Olivares
Santiago de Cuba, 1949. Poet, literary critic, and visual artist. He graduated with a degree in Painting from the Havana Art Institute in 1987. Beginning in 1971 and for more than three decades he was a professor of visual arts in different Cuban academies and at the Institute of Fine Arts in Medellín, Colombia. He has lived in Seville, Spain since 2003. Poetry: *Papeles personales* (1985, David Prize), *Cosas*

para seguir viviendo (1985, in *Seis a la mesa*), *A imagen y semejanza* (1987, 13 de Marzo Prize), *Caja de pandora* (1987), *Examen del guerrero* (1992, Jaime Gil de Biedma Prize), *Me llamo Antoine Doinel* (1992), *Proyecto para tiempos futuros* (1993), *Cristo entrando en Bruselas* (1994, Rafael Alberti Prize), *Lapislázuli* (1999), *Háblame de las ciudades perdidas* (1999, Renacimiento Prize), *El rostro y la máscara* (2000, Critics' Prize), *Últimos instantes de la víctima* (2001), and *Los poemas del Rey David* (2008). The poetry of Pérez Olivares – like the other authors found in the anthologies *Cuba: en su lugar la poesía* (1982), *Usted es la culpable* (1985), and *El pasado del cielo: La nueva y novísima poesía cubana* (1994) – isn't political but ethical. It stands out for its legitimization of the intellectual subject, marginalized by the neo-Stalinist politics in its heyday during the seventies. Furthermore, this poetry isn't limited to witness but encompasses the experiences of others – represented by the biographies of his intellectual heroes, mainly visual artists, like the author himself.

Soleida Ríos

Santiago de Cuba, 1950. Poet and literary critic. She studied History at the University of Oriente. She directed the José María Heredia literary workshop and was the founder and director of the Cultural Workshop, both in her native city. She has taught and promoted literature for more than three decades at diverse Cuban institutions. She has been awarded the Distinction for National Culture in 1996, among other honours. Poetry: *De la Sierra* (1977), *De pronto, abril* (1979), *Entre mundo y juguete* (1987), *El libro roto* (1994 and 2002), *Libro cero* (1998), *El libro de los sueños* (1999), *El texto sucio* (1999), and *Fuga: Una antología personal* (2004). Ríos expressly participates in the process of moving beyond conversational poetry and above all anti-poetry, her generation's resolve. A rarely studied aspect of this change, present in the author's first books, is the representation of the peasant world and island nature. Still, what's most relevant about this renovation of dialogic poetry is, with regard to content, the wider, deeper vision of society, attentive to once sidestepped public and personal conflicts, and as for form, the greatest tropological density and care with verse and language. Yet, Ríos does not linger here and her poetry increasingly questions the limits of genre, mostly opening toward narrative, without avoiding the other or leaving behind social intervention.

Reina María Rodríguez
Havana, 1952. Poet, prose writer, editor, and cultural promoter. She studied Spanish American Literature at the University of Havana. She directs the cultural space and publishing project Torre de Letras. She has received the Order for National Culture (1988); the Mexican journal *Plural*'s Poetry Prize (1990); France's Order of Arts and Letters, Chevalier (1999), Cuba's Alejo Carpentier Medal (2002) and National Literature Prize (2013), and Chile's Pablo Neruda Prize (2014), among other honours. Poetry: *La gente de mi barrio* (1976, 13 de Marzo Prize), *Cuando una mujer no duerme* (1980, Julián del Casal Prize), *Para un cordero blanco* (1984, Casa de las Américas Prize), *En la arena de Padua* (1992, Critics' Prize), *Páramos* (1995, Julián del Casal Prize and Critics' Prize), *Travelling* (1995), *La foto del invernadero* (1998, Casa de las Américas Prize and Critics' Prize), *Te daré de comer como a los pájaros* (2000, Critics' Prize), *Ellas escriben cartas de amor* (2002, anthology), *Otras cartas a Milena* (2004), *El libro de las clientas* (2005), *Bosque negro* (2005), *Catch and Release* (2007, Critics' Prize), *Variedades de Galiano* (2008), and *Las fotos de la señora Loss* (2010). Rodríguez's poetry is groundbreaking in the transition from colloquialism and anti-poetry to new forms of dialogic poetry in Cuba. In this process prevails the lyrical over the epic, the implicit message over the explicit, tropological language over prosaicism. Later on, Rodríguez's poetry becomes more experimental, aware of itself, yet never turning to solipsism.

Alex Fleites
Caracas, Venezuela, 1954. Poet, prose writer, literary critic, editor, journalist, and screenwriter. He received his degree in Philology from the University of Havana. He has been a writer for the newspaper *Juventud Rebelde* and the journals *El Caimán Barbudo* and *Cine Cubano*. He has directed the Ministry of Culture's Centre for Cinematographic Information. Poetry: *Primeros argumentos* (1974), *Dictado por la lluvia* (1976), *A dos espacios* (1983, Julián del Casal Prize), *El arca de la serena alegría* (1985, 13 de Marzo Prize), *De vital importancia* (1989, anthology), *Memorias del sueño* (1991), *El asesino de la mujer que pasa* (1993), *Ómnibus de noche* (1995), *Un perro en la casa del amor* (2003), and *La violenta ternura* (2006, anthology, prologue by Arturo Arango). Like others from his generation, Fleites breaks with colloquialism's extreme prosaicism by means of a more serene expression that privileges crafting of the verse. In this

readjustment of dialogic poetry, the representation of the quotidian surpasses the anecdotal, the description of an experience stands out, the immediate is approached in a more complex way. The work turns to the invention of reality, but always controlled by rationality, never as a radical break with order. Like in Cuban society at the end of the twentieth century, in Fleites' poetry original serenity has ceded its place to chaos, to the decentering of the poetic subject and its failed encounter with reality.

Víctor Rodríguez Núñez
Havana, 1955. Poet, journalist, critic, translator, and university professor. He received his Ph.D. in Hispanic Literatures from the University of Texas at Austin and teaches at Kenyon College, United States. In the eighties he was writer and Chief Editor for the cultural journal *El Caimán Barbudo*. Poetry: *Cayama* (1979), *Con raro olor a mundo* (1981, David Prize), *Noticiario del solo* (1987, *Plural* Prize), *Cuarto de desahogo* (1993), *Los poemas de nadie y otros poemas* (1994), *El último a la feria* (1995, EDUCA Prize), *Oración inconclusa* (2000, Renacimiento Prize), *Actas de medianoche I* (2006), *Actas de medianoche II* (2007, Leonor Prize), *tareas* (2011, Rincón de la Victoria Prize), *reversos* (2011), *deshielos* (2013), *desde un granero rojo* (2013, Alfons el Magnànim Prize), and *despegues* (Loewe Prize, 2016). His Selected Poems has appeared in Chinese, English, French, German, Italian, Macedonian, Serbian, and Swedish. He has compiled three anthologies that defined his generation, in addition to *La poesía del siglo XX en Cuba* (Madrid, 2011). In collaboration with Katherine M. Hedeen he has translated poetry from both English into Spanish (Mark Strand, John Kinsella) and Spanish into English (Juan Gelman, José Emilio Pacheco). He states that he has always sought 'poetry that is autonomous but not disengaged; participative but not political; subjective but not intimist; structured but not hermetic; communicative but not explicit; lyrical, but not ahistorical; dialogical, but not colloquial; Cuban but not from Cubanity or Cubanness; open to the world, but not colonized.'

Ángel Escobar
Guantánamo, 1957-Havana, 1997. Poet, prose writer, playwright, and essayist. He graduated in Performing Arts from the Havana Art Institute. Poetry: *Viejas palabras de uso* (1978, David Prize), *Epílogo famoso* (1985, Roberto Branly Prize), *Allegro de sonata* (1987), *La vía*

pública (1987), *Malos pasos* (1991), *Todavía* (1991), *Abuso de confianza* (1992), *Cuando salí de La Habana* (1996), *El examen no ha terminado* (1997), *La sombra del decir* (1997), *Fatiga ser dos sombras* (2002, anthology, prologue by Efraín Rodríguez Santana), and *Poesía completa* (2006, anthology, prologue by Enrique Saínz). Escobar's work is one of the most singular in Cuban poetry from the end of the twentieth century. From his first books, there is a shift dictated not only by aesthetic journeys but also for vital reasons. In a fierce confrontation with madness that ends in suicide, the poet expresses a tangled relationship with reality, which demands, in its representation, a progressive dismantling of discourse. Despite these displacements of meaning, a worldview remains, which does not appeal to transcendentalism as it radically doubts autonomy and the coherence of the 'I', along with a certainty about otherness that ultimately determines it; a conception of poetry as an intervention in reality.

Ramón Fernández-Larrea

Bayamo, 1958. Poet, comedian and writer for film, television, and radio. He studied History at the Havana Pedagogical Institute. For many years, his *Programa de Ramón* on *Radio Ciudad de La Habana* had a large audience. He went into exile in Spain, and currently lives in the United States where he writes comedies for television. He has received the cultural magazine *Revolución y Cultura*'s Poetry Prize, among other honours. Poetry: *El pasado del cielo* (1987, Julián del Casal Prize), *Poemas para ponerse en la cabeza* (1989, *El Caimán Barbudo*Prize), *El libro de las instrucciones* (1991), *Manual de pasión* (1993), *El libro de los salmos feroces* (1994), *Terneros que nunca mueran de rodillas* (1998, Julio Tovar Prize), *Cantar del tigre ciego* (2001), *Nunca canté en Broadway* (2005), and *Todos los cielos del cielo (*the Gastón Baquero International Poetry Prize, 2014).Fernández Larrea's poetry proposes to recognize the autonomy and the critical capacity of the artist and their work. The cover of *El pasado del cielo* warns we are before a poetry made to 'discuss, to move, to not stay still before impeccable arpeggios, but angry and imperfect, sealed by the urgency of living.' Standouts include the violence of tropological associations, a hyperbolic and at times melodramatic character, and deliberately shocking language. The poet must overtake the limits of conversational poetry to realize a definitively utopian subversion of values.

Roberto Méndez
Camagüey, 1958. Poet, essayist, prose writer, literary and art critic, and journalist. He graduated with a degree in Sociology from the University of Havana and a doctorate in Art Sciences from the Havana Art Institute. He worked more than a decade in his birth city as a social researcher. Member of the Cuban Academy of the Spanish Language. With his essays he has won the Critics' Prize on three separate occasions. Poetry: *Carta de relación* (1988), *Manera de estar solo* (1989), *Desayuno sobre la hierba con máscaras* (1991 and 1993), *Conversación con el ciervo* (1994), *Música de cámara para los delfines* (1995), *Soledad en la Plaza de la Vigía* (1995), *Cuaderno de Aliosha* (2000 and 2007), *Viendo acabado tanto reino fuerte* (2001, Nicolás Guillén Prize and Critics' Prize), *Libro del invierno* (2002), *Autorretrato con cardo* (2004, personal anthology), *Las especies del aire* (2005), and *El rostro* (2007). Méndez's work distances itself from both colloquialism and anti-poetry, yet does not give up a dialogue with reality, and in its course intervenes to recreate it. Though its Catholicism brings it closer to the tradition of *Orígenes*, it always keeps its expressive personality, its authenticity in the quest for knowledge, understood as the coming together of culture and experience, idea and emotion. As in the cases of García-Marruz and Friol, Méndez's poetry is dialogic above all due to its identification with others.

Sigfredo Ariel
Santa Clara, 1962. Poet, prose writer, essayist, visual artist, music producer, scriptwriter for film, television, and radio. He studied at the Havana Art Institute. For more than two decades he has worked for Cuban radio and television, writing and directing cultural programs. He was the musical consultant for the Wim Wender's film *Buena Vista Social Club* (1998) and the producer of numerous albums of Cuban popular music. Currently, he directs the UNEAC's journal *Revista de Música Cubana*. He has received the *El Caimán Barbudo* Prize (1985 and 1988), the Abril Prize (1990), the International ULCRA Prize for Latin American Audiovisuals (Mexico, 1990), *La Gaceta de Cuba* Prize (1995), the Best Unpublished Script from the Havana Film Festival (1997), and the Distinction for National Culture (1997), among other honours. Poetry: *La imprenta* (1985), *Algunos pocos conocidos* (1987, David Prize), *Manualidades* (1988), *El enorme verano* (1995, Pinos Nuevos Prize), *El cielo imaginario* (1996), *Las primeras itálicas* (1997), *Hotel Central* (1998, Julián del Casal Prize), *Los peces*

& *La vida tropical* (2000), *Manos a la obra* (2002, Nicolás Guillén Prize and Critics' Prize), *Escrito en Playa Amarilla* (2004), *Born in Santa Clara* (2006, Julián del Casal Prize and Critics' Prize), and *Cielo imaginario* (2008). In Ariel's work colloquial language reaches a notable refinement. It is poetry not absorbed by the personal, where what prevails is the affirmative attitude of social and cultural identification, but with no diminishing of a critical stance.

Juan Carlos Pérez Flores
Havana, 1962. Poet. Poetry: *Los pájaros escritos* (1994, David Prize and Critics' Prize), *Distintos modos de cavar un túnel* (2003, Julián del Casal Prize, prologue by Reina María Rodríguez), *El contragolpe (y otros poemas horizontales)* (2007 and 2009, prologue by Lizabel Mónica), and *Un hombre de la clase muerta* (2007, anthology, prologue by Reina María Rodríguez). Without sociological pretensions, Pérez Flores' poetry represents Cuba's deteriorated social and cultural reality, beginning in 1991, during the so-called Special Period. His poetic subject is marginalized, crossing the city from below, yet without making himself a victim or making concessions to solipsism. It is moving that this poetry continues, in the end, attempting a dialogue; and despite being critical, and perhaps because of it, does not take on negativity. It is also worthwhile to highlight that this discourse is not limited to social condemnation, and brings to light a notable expressive force, with a complex formal elaboration. Furthermore, the dialogic character of Flores' poetry becomes evident in the demand for an active reader, who can decode a precise, plain discourse, but where meanings accumulate, contradict one another, and are reiterated, and later become pluralized. In this way, Pérez's work, where idea and feeling, authenticity and formal rigor, are all connected, enriches Cuban participative poetry.

Alberto Rodríguez Tosca
Artemisa, 1962-Havana, 2015. Poet, prose writer, essayist, editor, university professor, scriptwriter and director of radio programs. He studied Film, Radio, and Television Directing at Havana's Art Institute. From his studio at *Radio Ciudad de La Habana* he achieved a notable dissemination of poetry. In 1994 he was awarded the National Journalism Prize and that same year he moved to Colombia. In that country he was an editor for various cultural publications (like *Suburbia Capital, Urbe, Horas, La Sagrada Escritura*), directed literary

Roberto Méndez

Camagüey, 1958. Poet, essayist, prose writer, literary and art critic, and journalist. He graduated with a degree in Sociology from the University of Havana and a doctorate in Art Sciences from the Havana Art Institute. He worked more than a decade in his birth city as a social researcher. Member of the Cuban Academy of the Spanish Language. With his essays he has won the Critics' Prize on three separate occasions. Poetry: *Carta de relación* (1988), *Manera de estar solo* (1989), *Desayuno sobre la hierba con máscaras* (1991 and 1993), *Conversación con el ciervo* (1994), *Música de cámara para los delfines* (1995), *Soledad en la Plaza de la Vigía* (1995), *Cuaderno de Aliosha* (2000 and 2007), *Viendo acabado tanto reino fuerte* (2001, Nicolás Guillén Prize and Critics' Prize), *Libro del invierno* (2002), *Autorretrato con cardo* (2004, personal anthology), *Las especies del aire* (2005), and *El rostro* (2007). Méndez's work distances itself from both colloquialism and anti-poetry, yet does not give up a dialogue with reality, and in its course intervenes to recreate it. Though its Catholicism brings it closer to the tradition of *Orígenes*, it always keeps its expressive personality, its authenticity in the quest for knowledge, understood as the coming together of culture and experience, idea and emotion. As in the cases of García-Marruz and Friol, Méndez's poetry is dialogic above all due to its identification with others.

Sigfredo Ariel

Santa Clara, 1962. Poet, prose writer, essayist, visual artist, music producer, scriptwriter for film, television, and radio. He studied at the Havana Art Institute. For more than two decades he has worked for Cuban radio and television, writing and directing cultural programs. He was the musical consultant for the Wim Wender's film *Buena Vista Social Club* (1998) and the producer of numerous albums of Cuban popular music. Currently, he directs the UNEAC's journal *Revista de Música Cubana*. He has received the *El Caimán Barbudo* Prize (1985 and 1988), the Abril Prize (1990), the International ULCRA Prize for Latin American Audiovisuals (Mexico, 1990), *La Gaceta de Cuba* Prize (1995), the Best Unpublished Script from the Havana Film Festival (1997), and the Distinction for National Culture (1997), among other honours. Poetry: *La imprenta* (1985), *Algunos pocos conocidos* (1987, David Prize), *Manualidades* (1988), *El enorme verano* (1995, Pinos Nuevos Prize), *El cielo imaginario* (1996), *Las primeras itálicas* (1997), *Hotel Central* (1998, Julián del Casal Prize), *Los peces*

& *La vida tropical* (2000), *Manos a la obra* (2002, Nicolás Guillén Prize and Critics' Prize), *Escrito en Playa Amarilla* (2004), *Born in Santa Clara* (2006, Julián del Casal Prize and Critics' Prize), and *Cielo imaginario* (2008). In Ariel's work colloquial language reaches a notable refinement. It is poetry not absorbed by the personal, where what prevails is the affirmative attitude of social and cultural identification, but with no diminishing of a critical stance.

Juan Carlos Pérez Flores
Havana, 1962. Poet. Poetry: *Los pájaros escritos* (1994, David Prize and Critics' Prize), *Distintos modos de cavar un túnel* (2003, Julián del Casal Prize, prologue by Reina María Rodríguez), *El contragolpe (y otros poemas horizontales)* (2007 and 2009, prologue by Lizabel Mónica), and *Un hombre de la clase muerta* (2007, anthology, prologue by Reina María Rodríguez). Without sociological pretensions, Pérez Flores' poetry represents Cuba's deteriorated social and cultural reality, beginning in 1991, during the so-called Special Period. His poetic subject is marginalized, crossing the city from below, yet without making himself a victim or making concessions to solipsism. It is moving that this poetry continues, in the end, attempting a dialogue; and despite being critical, and perhaps because of it, does not take on negativity. It is also worthwhile to highlight that this discourse is not limited to social condemnation, and brings to light a notable expressive force, with a complex formal elaboration. Furthermore, the dialogic character of Flores' poetry becomes evident in the demand for an active reader, who can decode a precise, plain discourse, but where meanings accumulate, contradict one another, and are reiterated, and later become pluralized. In this way, Pérez's work, where idea and feeling, authenticity and formal rigor, are all connected, enriches Cuban participative poetry.

Alberto Rodríguez Tosca
Artemisa, 1962-Havana, 2015. Poet, prose writer, essayist, editor, university professor, scriptwriter and director of radio programs. He studied Film, Radio, and Television Directing at Havana's Art Institute. From his studio at *Radio Ciudad de La Habana* he achieved a notable dissemination of poetry. In 1994 he was awarded the National Journalism Prize and that same year he moved to Colombia. In that country he was an editor for various cultural publications (like *Suburbia Capital*, *Urbe*, *Horas*, *La Sagrada Escritura*), directed literary

workshops at the Casa de Poesía Silva, and gave literature courses at Bogotá's Pontificia Universidad Javeriana. Poetry: *Todas las jaurías del Rey* (1987, David Prize), *Otros poemas* (1992, Critics' Prize), *El viaje* (2003), *Escrito sobre el hielo* (2006), and *Las derrotas* (2008). Rodríguez Tosca's poetry is one of the most profound representations of the exile experience, of the displacement suffered by more than a million Cubans since 1959. Instead of the poetic subject's negativity before reality, what is expressed is the negation of the negation that he is a victim, and so, what actually prevails is an affirmative attitude. In other words, he is not self-marginalized for opposing a social system but rather excluded for his condition as immigrant. Undoubtedly the real experience of modern society enriches his poetic perception, freeing it in the philosophical realm from solipsism and in the ideological realm from liberal fantasies.

Carlos Augusto Alfonso
Havana, 1963. He studied Biology and History at the University of Havana. Poetry: *El segundo aire* (1987, David Prize), *Población flotante* (1994), *La Oración de Letrán* (1996), *Fast Delivery* (1997), *Cabeza abajo* (1998, Julián del Casal Prize and Critics' Prize), and *Cerval* (2001 and 2004, Raúl Hernández Novás Prize). Alfonso's poetry offers one of the most radical positions in contemporary Cuban literature. He keeps his predecessors' interest in the quotidian, but rather than celebrate it, he expresses discomfort, an estrangement that has its roots in the current crisis in Cuban society. Still, he does not limit himself to the representation of the immediate, since his notion of reality is quite vast and complex, with a notable richness and diversity. What is offered in this poetry – which leaves behind an expression of personal experiences and hence distances itself from solipsism – is a simultaneous, multilateral perception of the world. Here, past, present, and future are relative, they contradict one other only in appearance, more than once they are juxtaposed; history is not linear, everything can happen at the same time, in a dialectic that doesn't recognize hierarchies. The less relatable contexts are superimposed, even to a certain point they compliment one another, from Arthurian legend to international politics, without transcendentalist solutions. Alfonso's poetic subject is always attentive, vigilant of what is happening, though he may not make it explicit, his social intervention is subtle but firm.

Ricardo Alberto Pérez
Havana, 1963. Poet, essayist, literary critic, and translator. He has received the *La Gaceta de Cuba* Prize (2003) and the Nosside Caribe Prize (2005), among other honours. Poetry: *Geanot (el otro ruido de la noche)* (1993 and 2000, Critics' Prize), *Nietzsche dibuja a Cósima Wagner* (1996), *Turín sin pájaro, sin reloj* (2000), *Trillos urbanos* (2003), *Vibraciones del buey* (2003), *Oral-B* (2007, Nicolás Guillén Prize), and *Los tuberculosos y otros poemas: Antología personal* (2007, prologue by Reina María Rodríguez). Pérez was one of the protagonists of the revolt in Cuban poetry in the eighties, and is one of the few who has managed to create solid, thriving work. With his singular poetic language, which rejects traditional beauty and seeks to desanctify without adopting any pose, this author assumes a postmodern sensibility and reaches a balance between the neo-barroque and neo-realism. In this way, Pérez's poetic subject takes on a peripheral social position; yet he doesn't remove his gaze from reality, and that gaze is essentially questioning. He seeks to defamiliarize the quotidian, inciting not to act simply out of reflex, he undoubtedly wants to make us aware, give us agency. Ultimately, Pérez's splendid work is inscribed, as that of the best poets of his generation, in the dialectic negation of a dialogic poetry, a critical affirmation of this fundamental aspect of Cuban poetry from the second half of the twentieth century.

Omar Pérez López
Havana, 1964. Poet, essayist, journalist, and translator. He received his degree in English Language and Literature from the University of Havana. He was a writer for *El Caimán Barbudo*. He lived in Holland and traveled through Europe for some years, dedicated to learning languages like Dutch and Italian. Poetry: *Algo de lo sagrado* (1996), *¿Oíste hablar del gato de pelea?* (1999), *Canciones y letanías* (2002), *Lingua franca* (2009), and *Crítica de la razón puta* (2009, Nicolás Guillén Prize). Pérez López's first collection is one of the great works of dialogic poetry in Cuba. It represents, with its rebellious yet affirmative spirit and strong ethics, the crisis of the island's society and culture brought about by the fall of European socialism, the American embargo, and internal errors. In later books this poetics, which despite an experimental character emphasizes continuity over rupture, drifted toward mysticism and the exploration of language under the influence of Buddhism and the knowledge of other

languages. Pérez López's opting for Buddhism, quite rare in Cuban poetry, reiterates the identification with the other, making it free from the harm of solipsism; this alongside the incorporation of other languages in the poetic discourse expresses recognition of otherness, of writing as dialogue.

Damaris Calderón

Havana, 1967. Poet, essayist, editor, children's writer, and visual artist. She studied Philology at the University of Havana, and Classic Languages and Literatures at the Universidad Metropolitana de Ciencias de la Educación in Santiago de Chile. In Cuba, she worked as an instructor in the amateur artists movement, and in Chile, where she's lived since 1995, she founded the publisher Las Dos Fridas, and is a university professor. She has received the *Revolución y Cultura* Poetry Prize and the Guggenheim Fellowship (2011), among other honours. Poetry: *Con el terror del equilibrista* (1987, Joven Poeta Prize), *Duras aguas del trópico* (1992), *Guijarros* (1994 and 1997), *Se adivina un país* (1999, poems for children, Ismaelillo Prize), *Duro de roer* (1999 and 2005), *Babosas: Dejando mi propio rastro* (1998), *Sílabas: Ecce homo* (2000, *Revista de Libros de El Mercurio* Prize), *Parloteo de sombra* (2004), *Los amores del mal* (2006 and 2010), and *La extranjera* (2007). Calderón's work does not opt to emphasize the signifier over the signified, to emphasize how to say something over saying it, and this is undoubtedly related to realism and the quest for communication. In this work there is also not avant-garde nostalgia, or manifestations of the neo-baroque. Above all there is not a return to solipsism, no matter how much anguish or pain is revealed. Its representation of the feminine condition, implicit and profound, includes the identification with the oppressed and repressed other.